Within the pages of this book you will find a variety of different Art Nouveau colouring designs for your own creativity. Simply relax, de-stress yourself and use your own imagination when colouring in these wonderful designs.

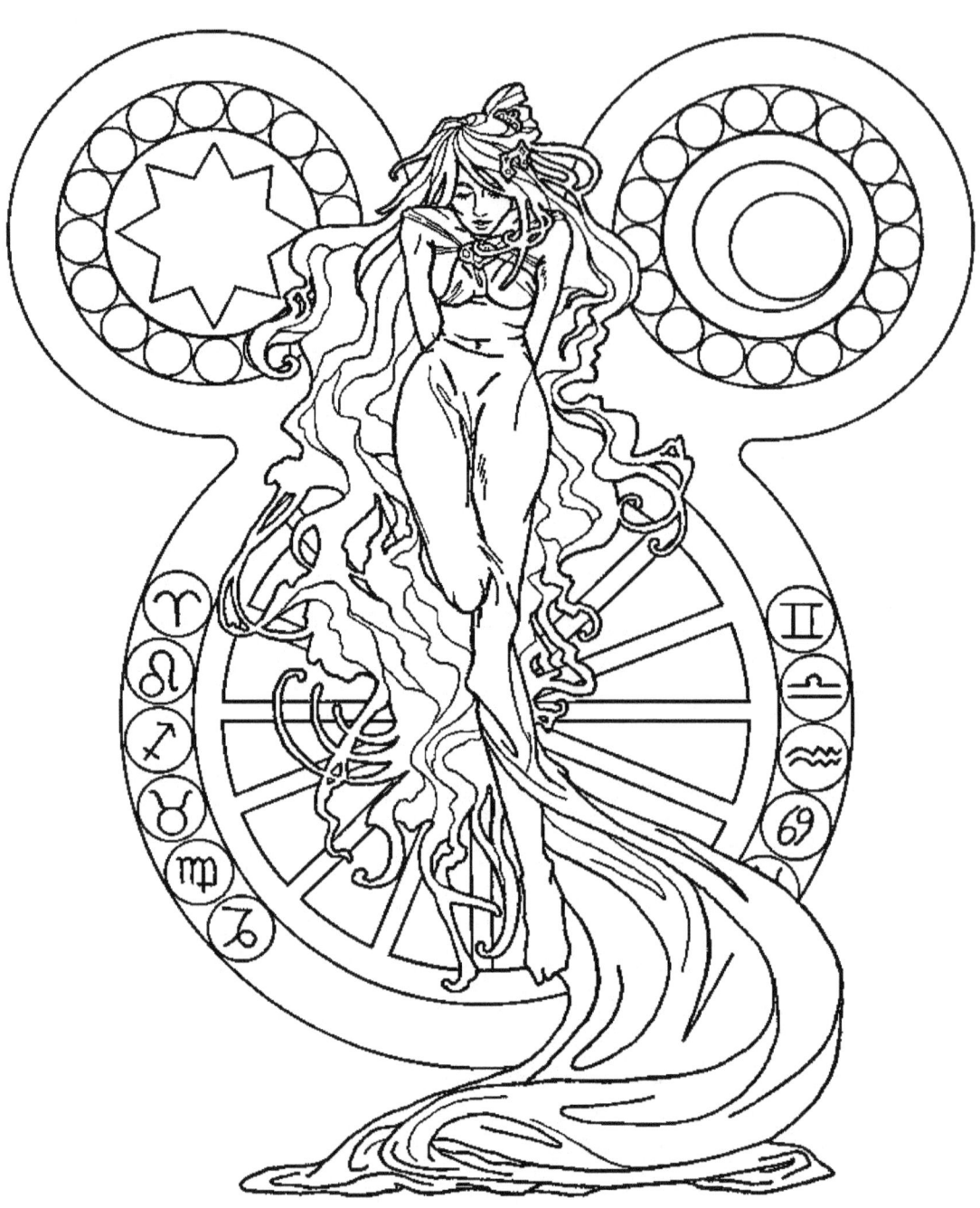

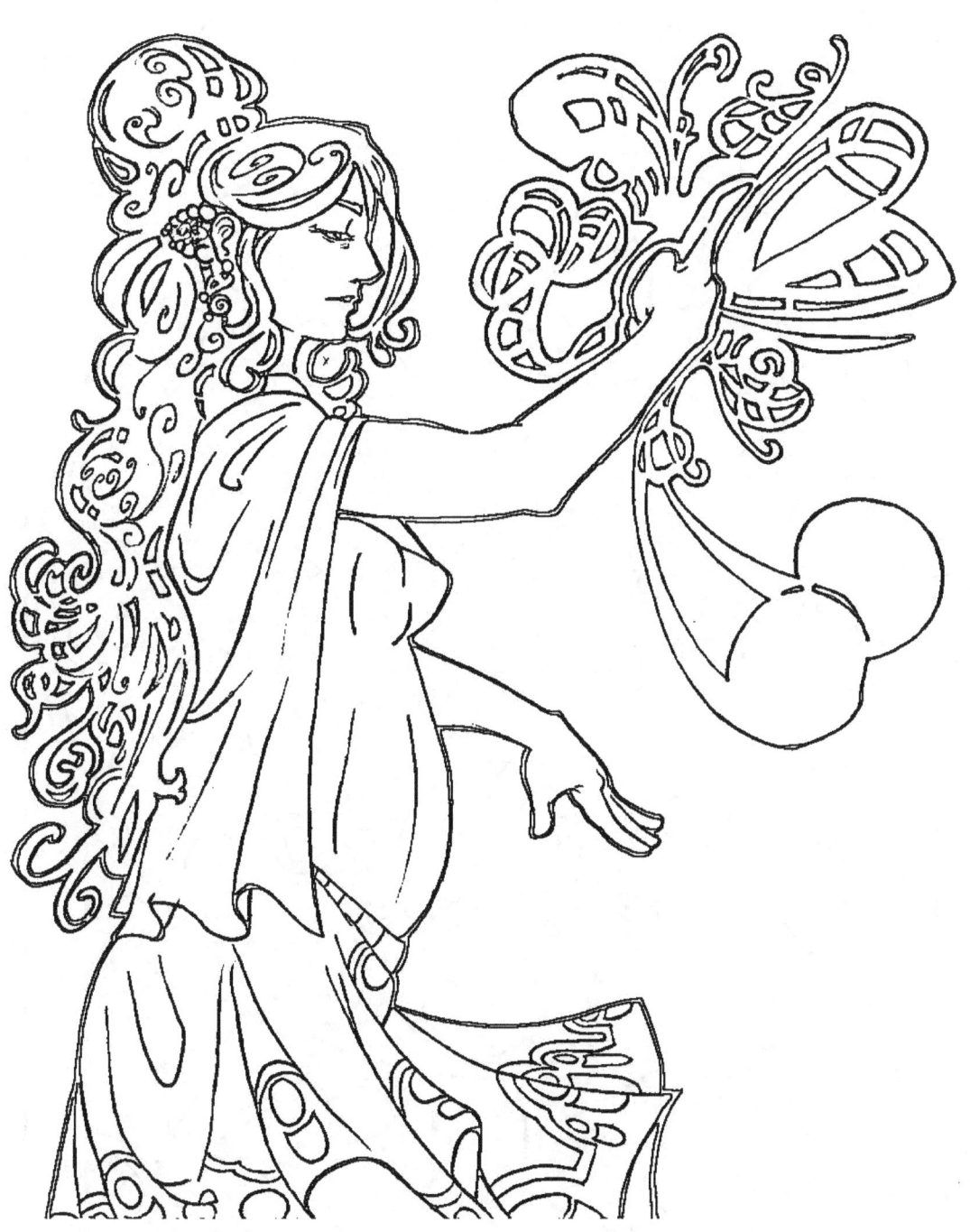

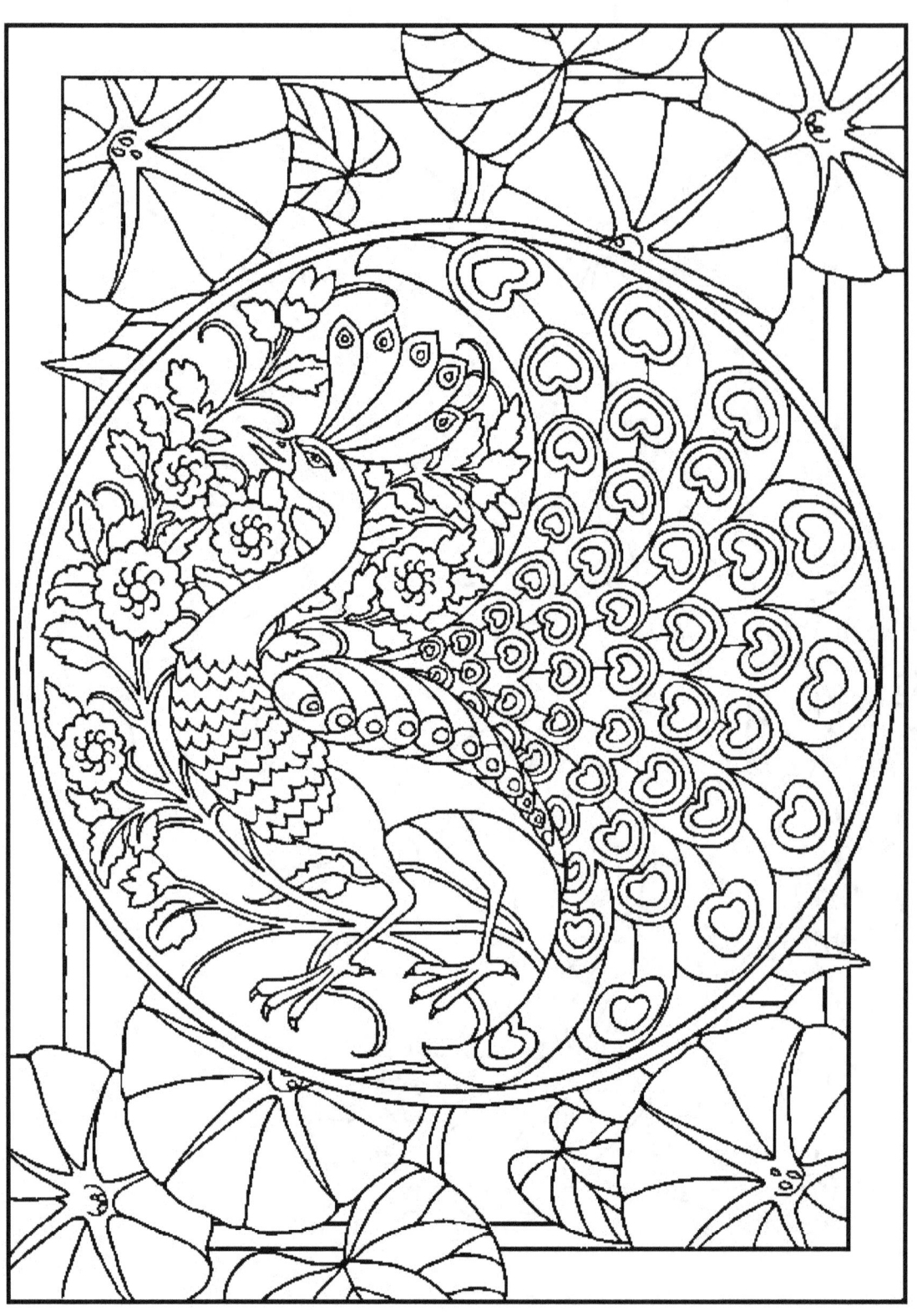

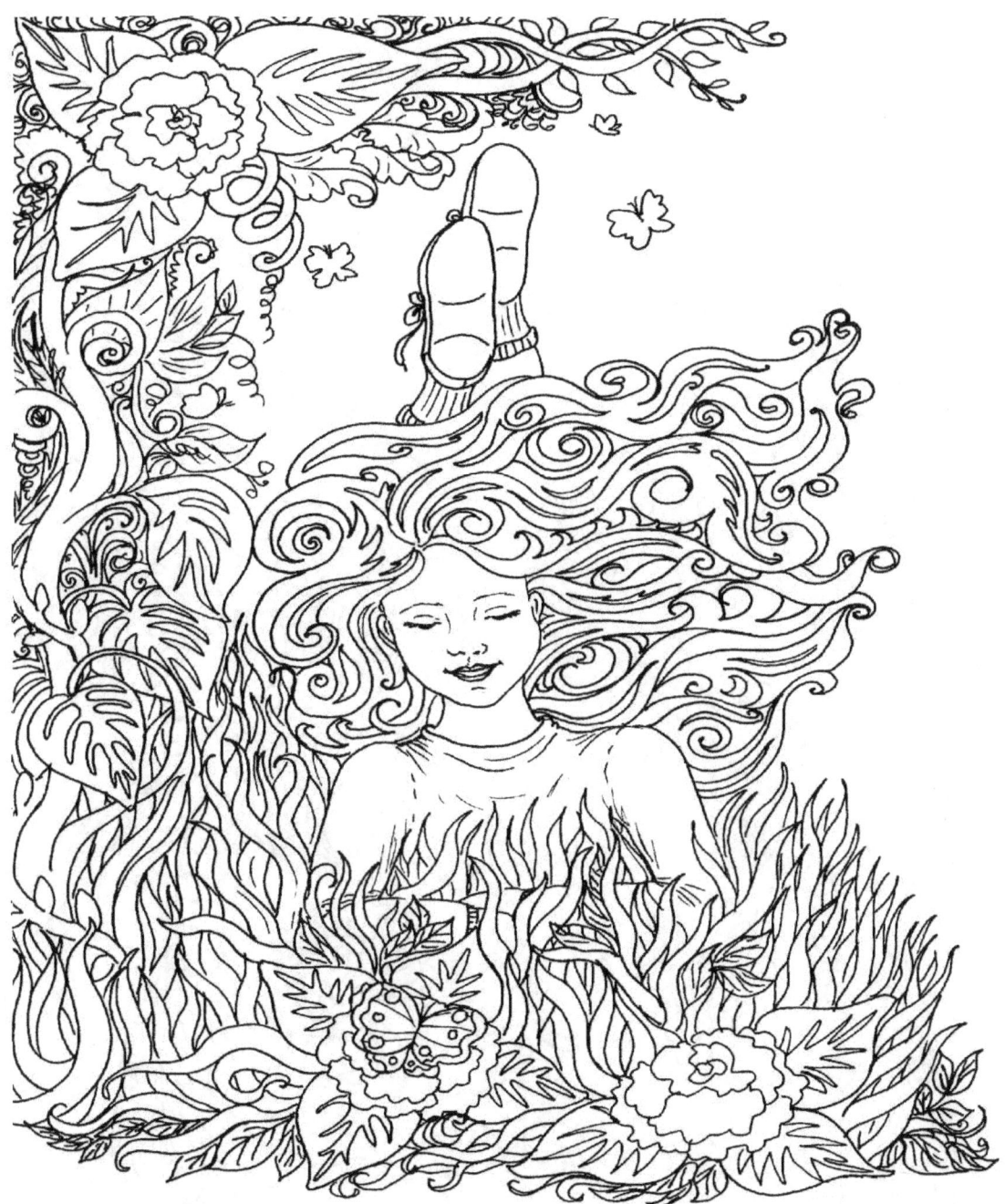

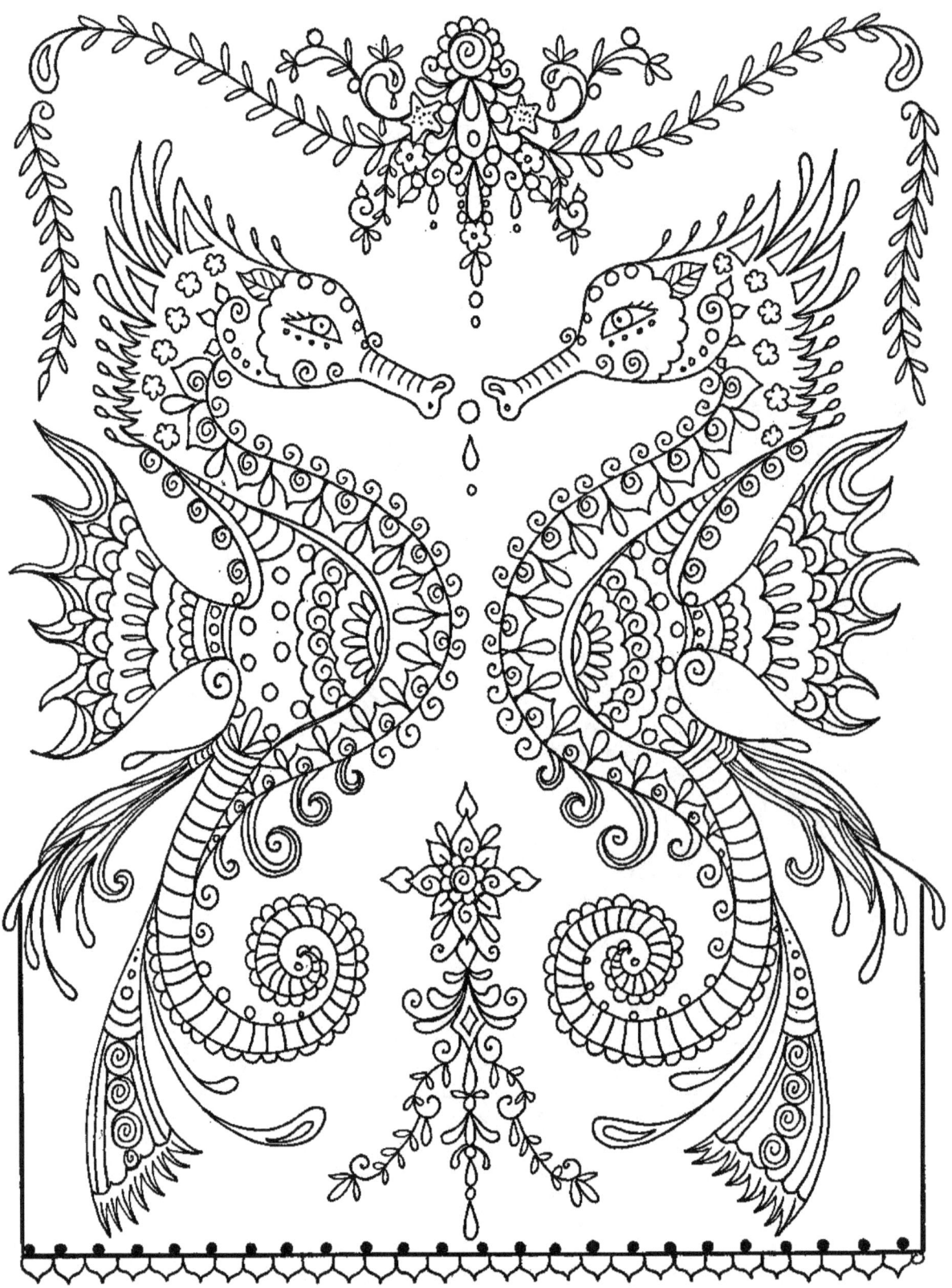

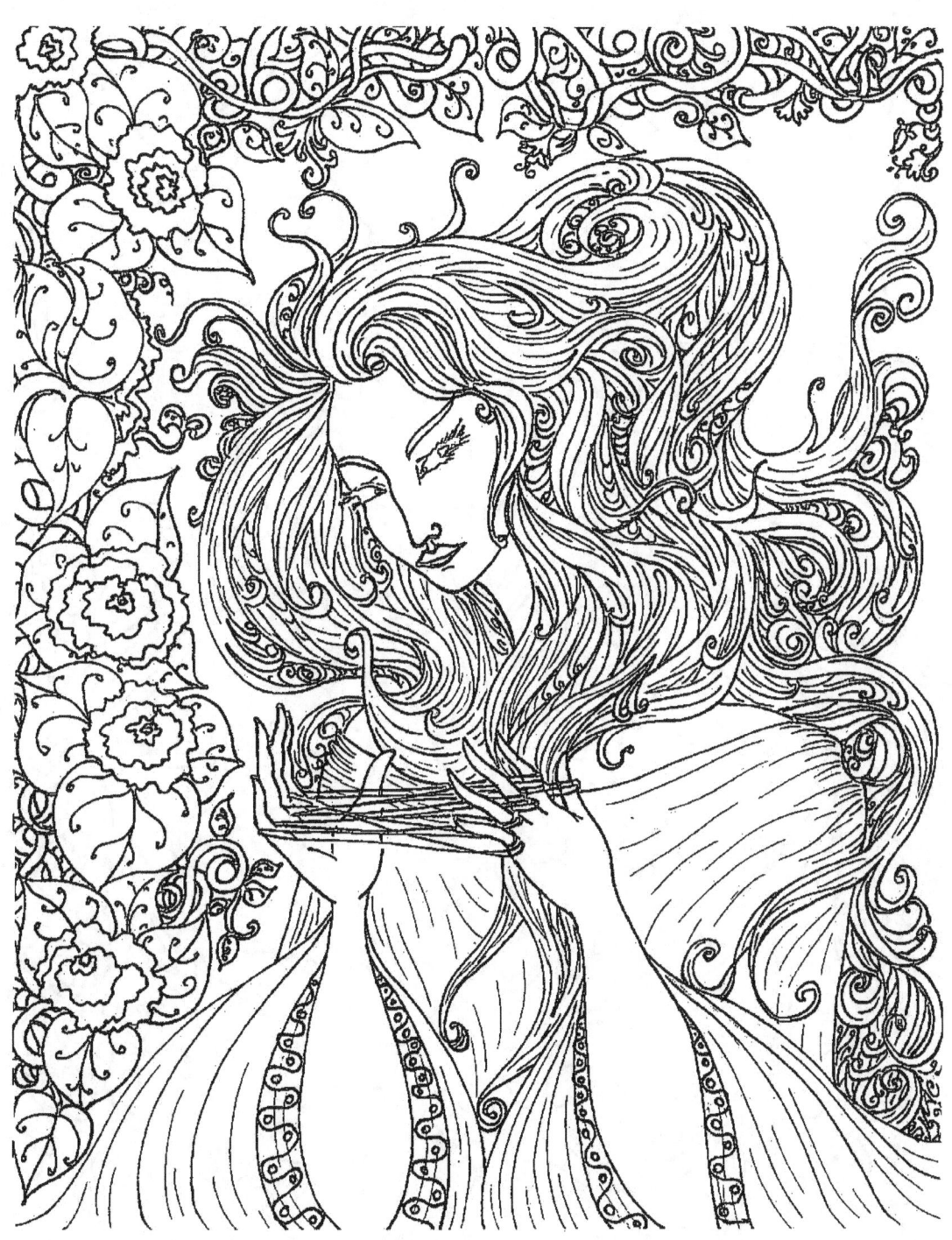

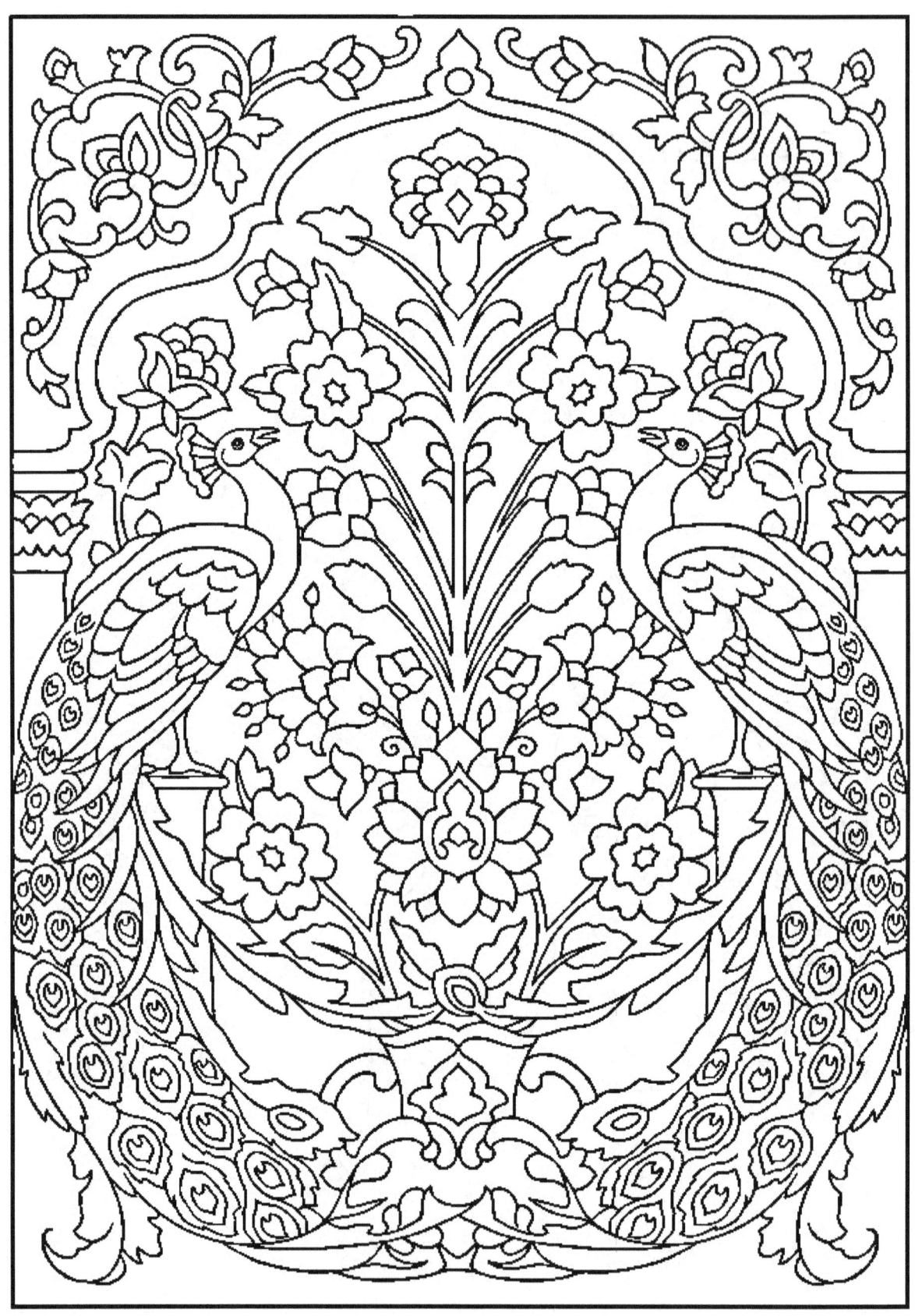

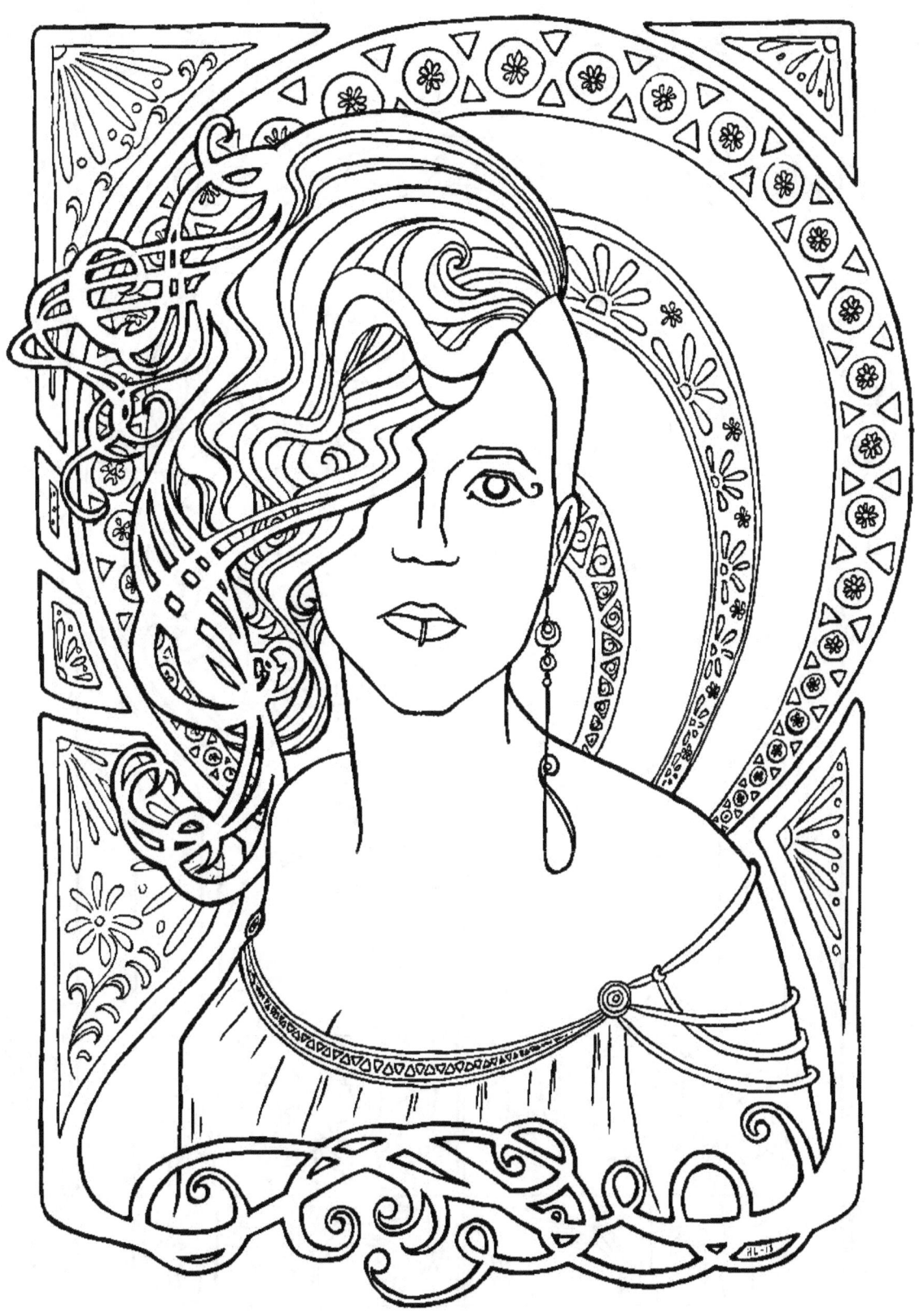

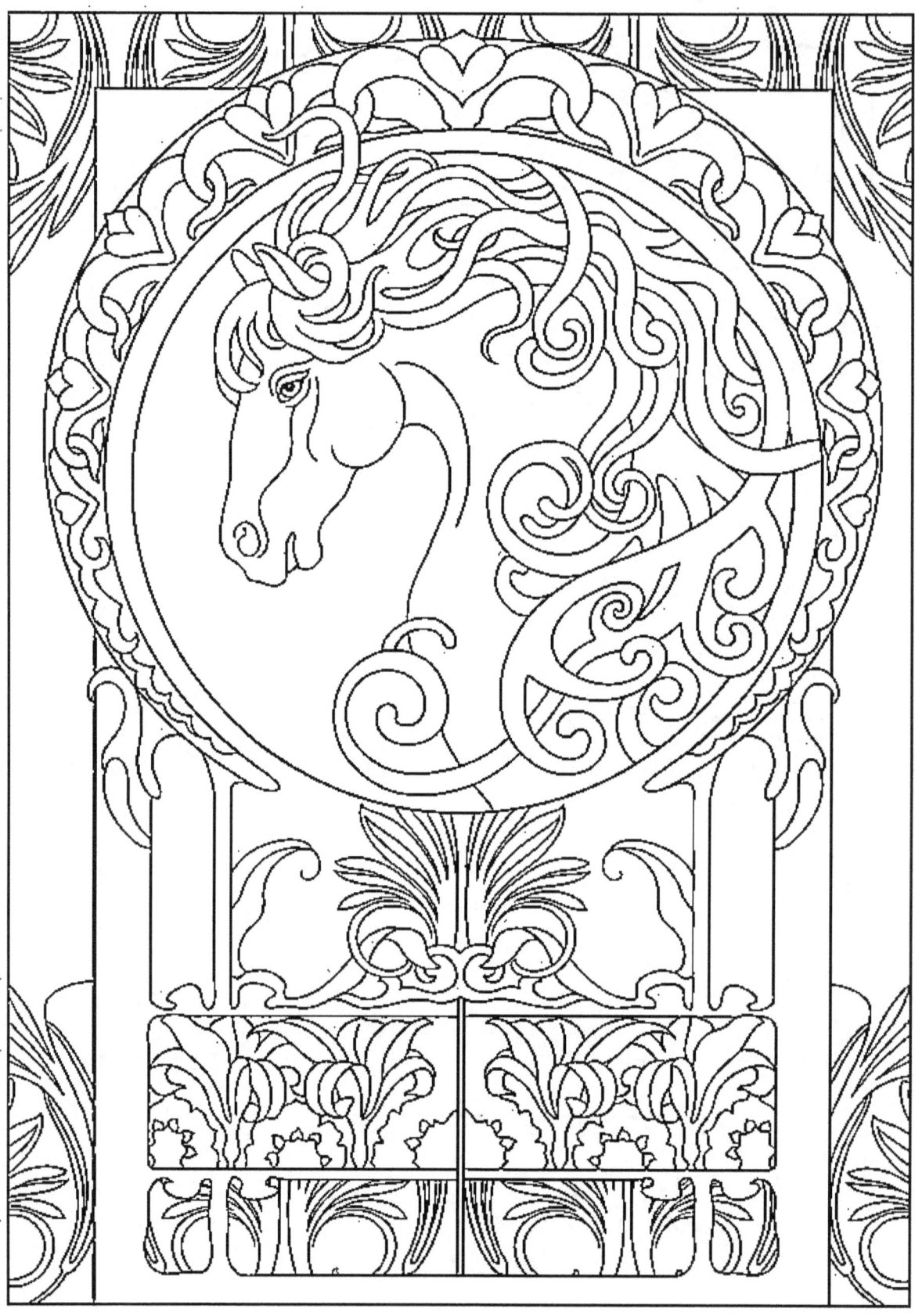

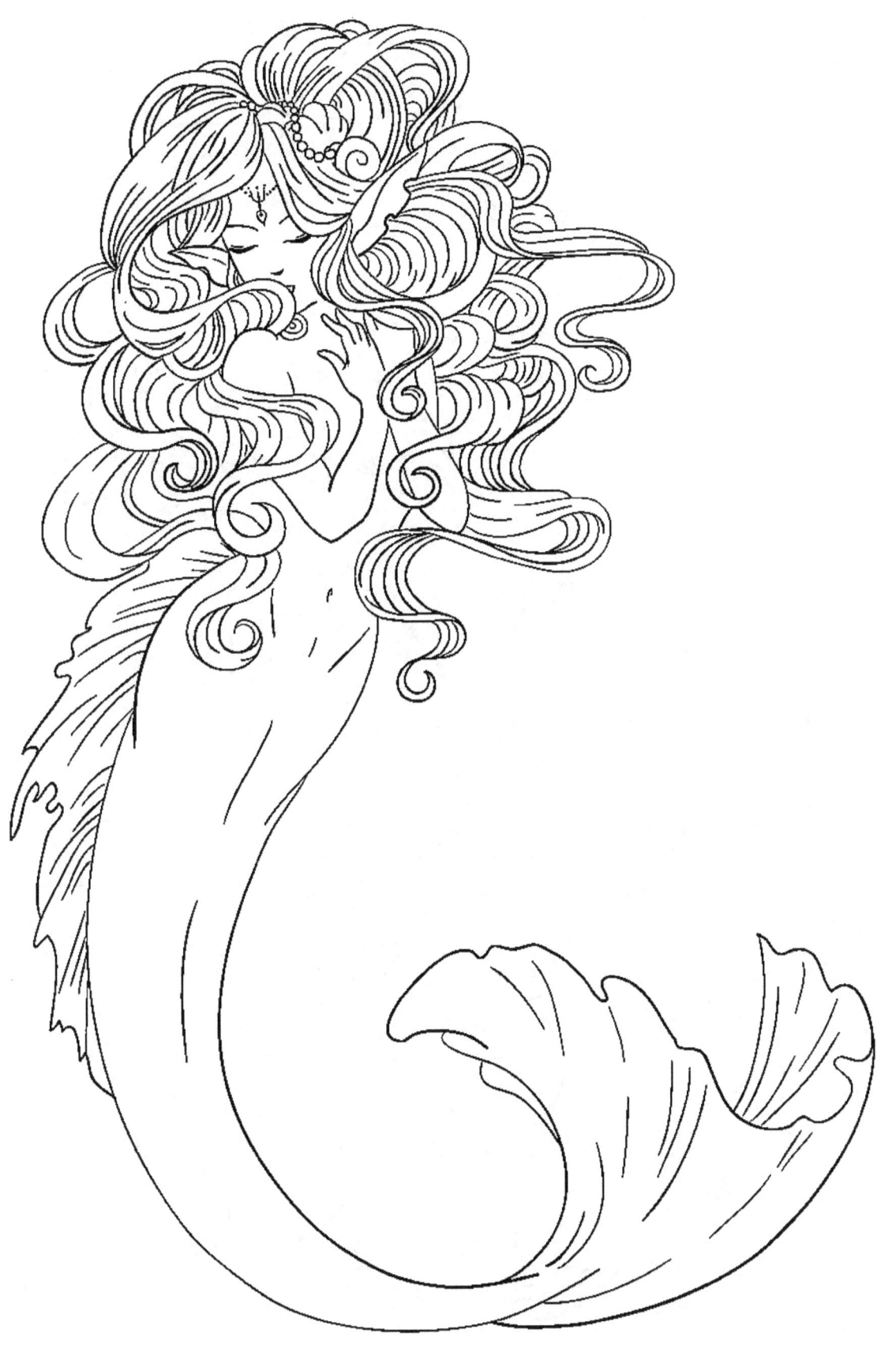

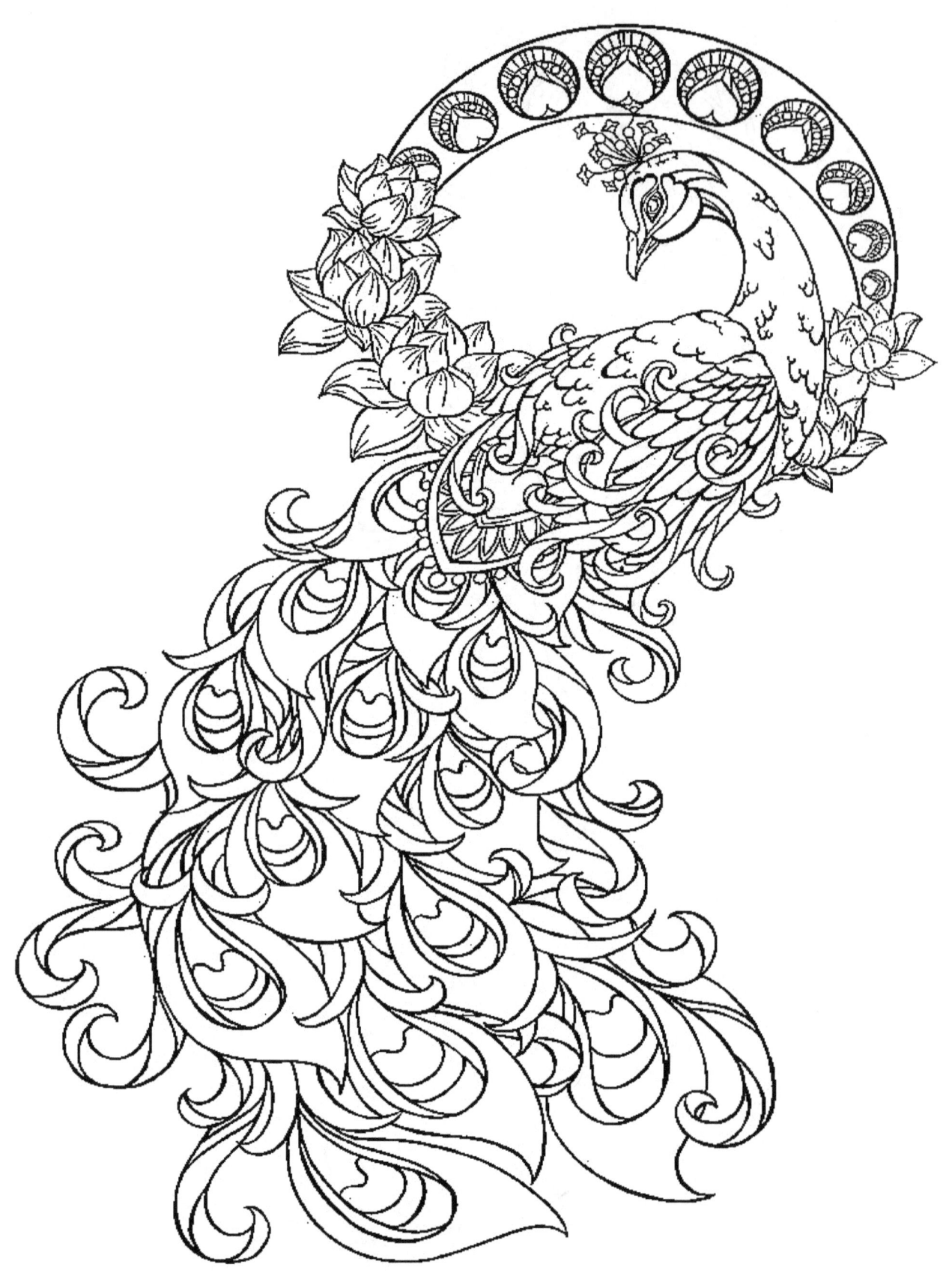

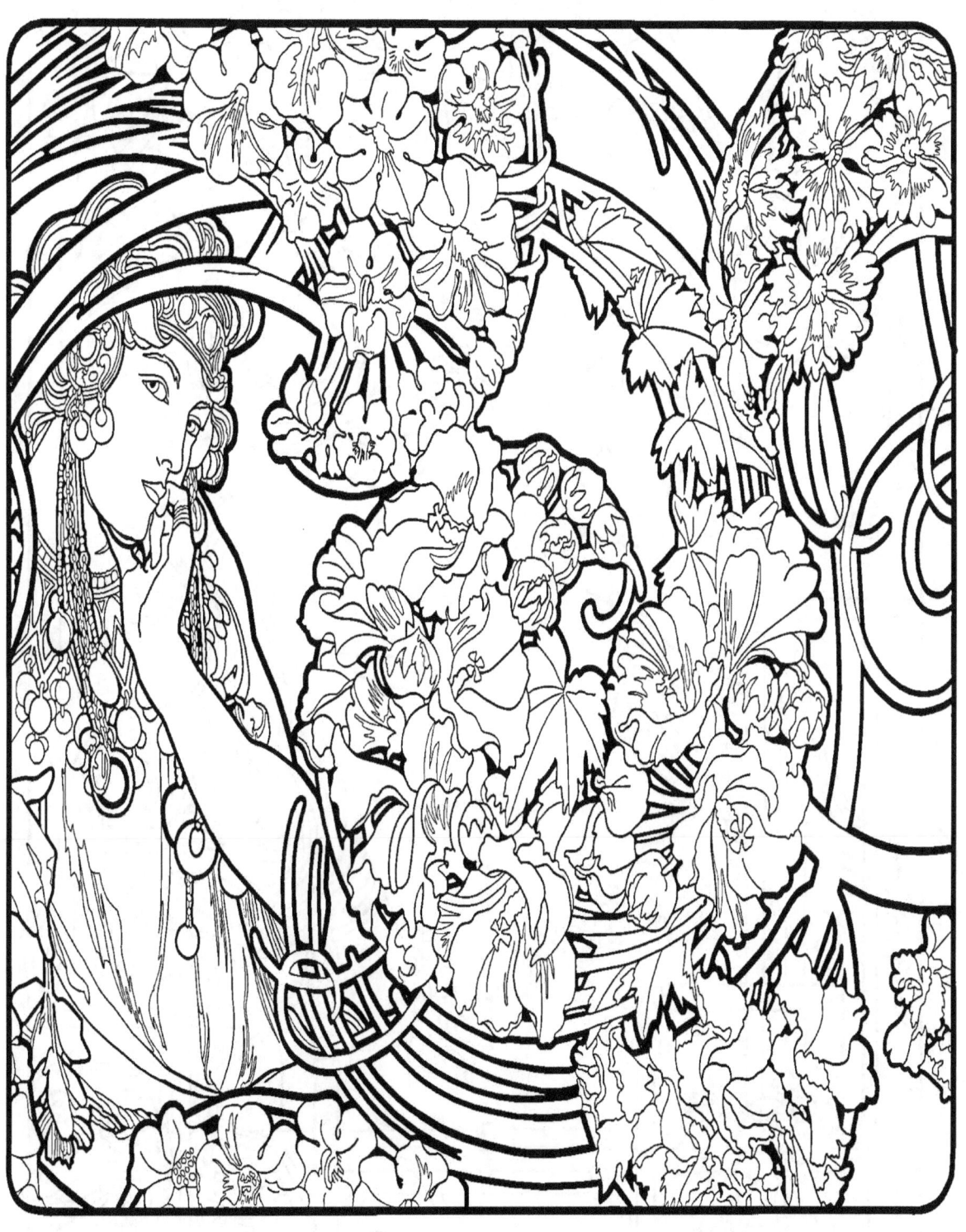

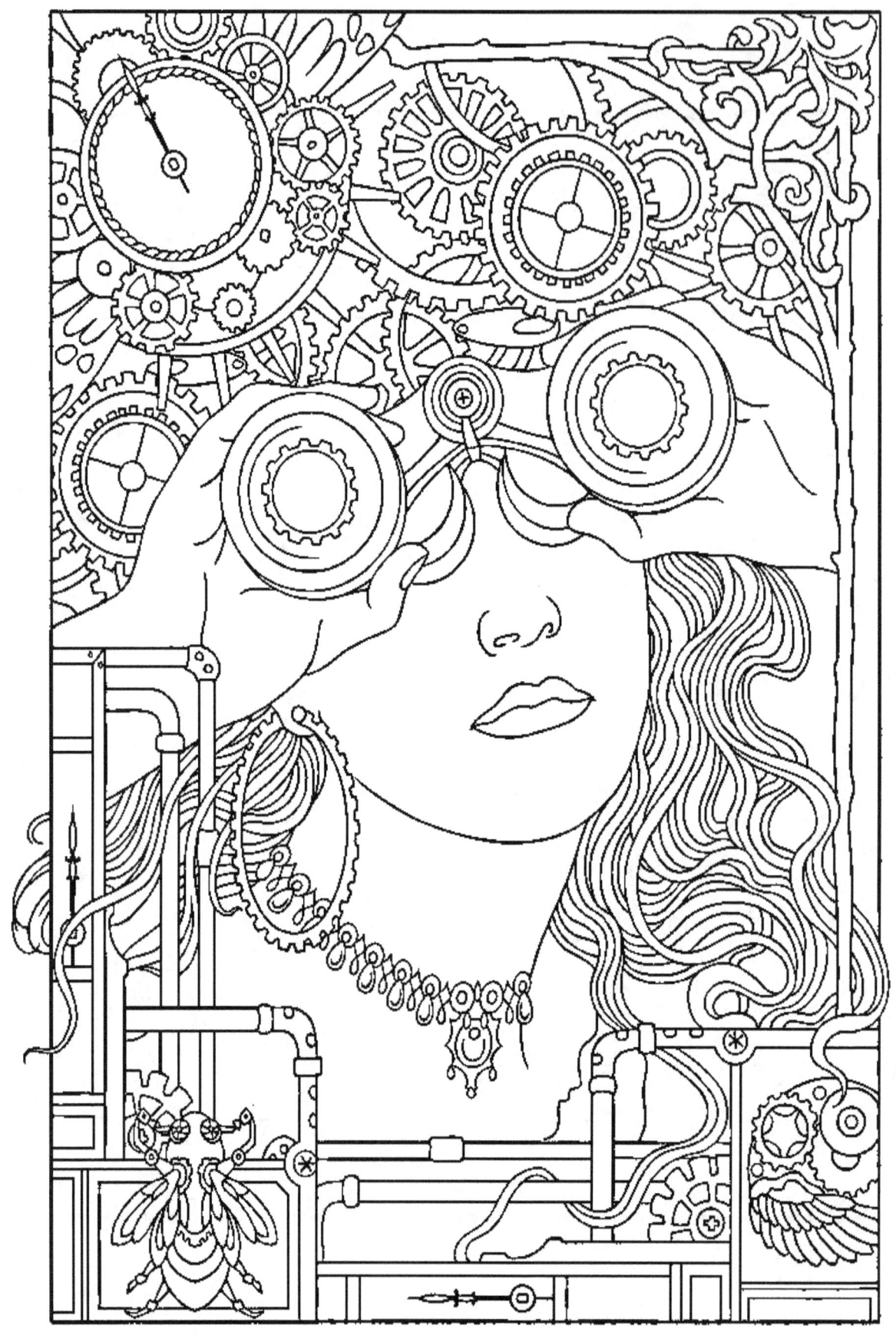

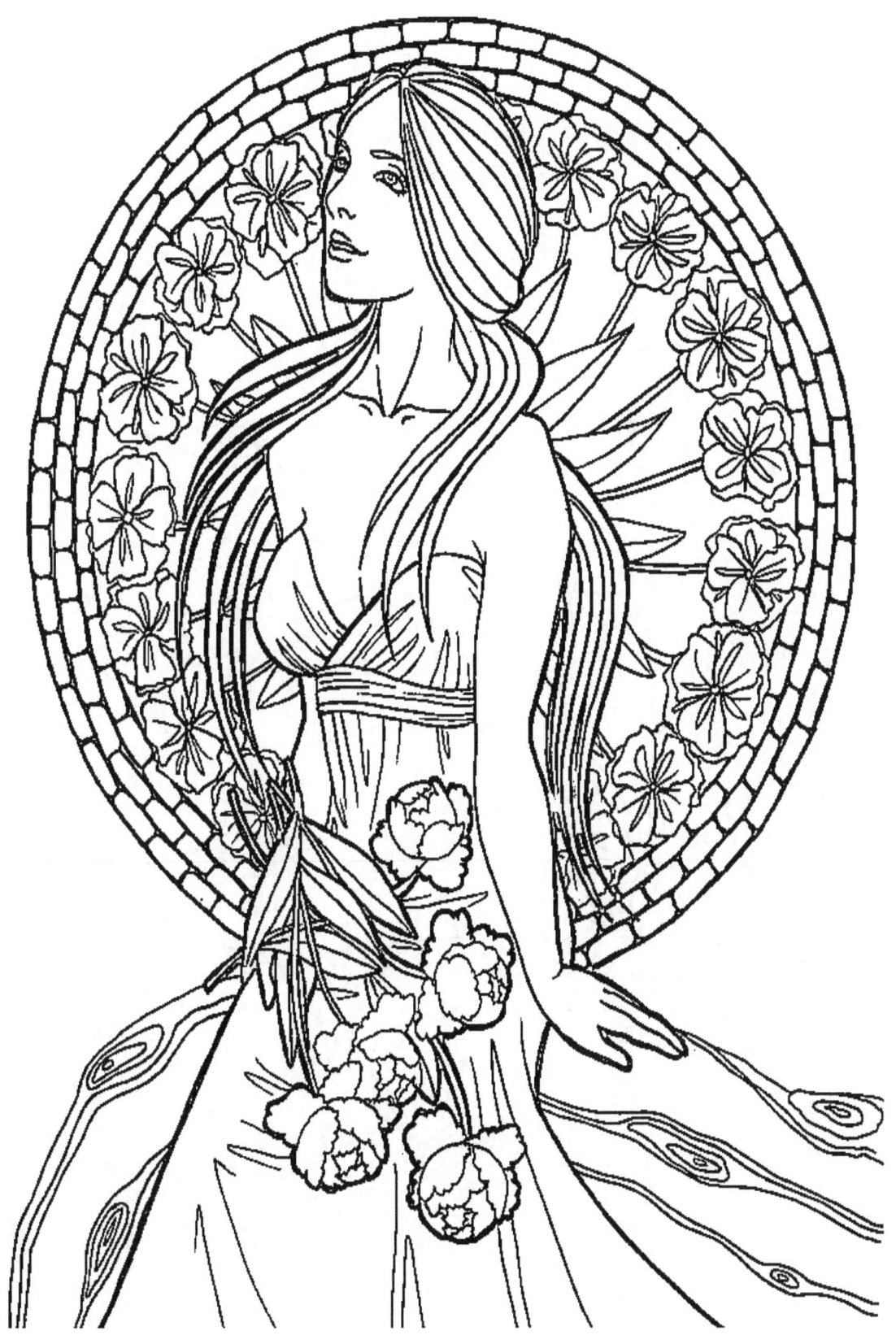

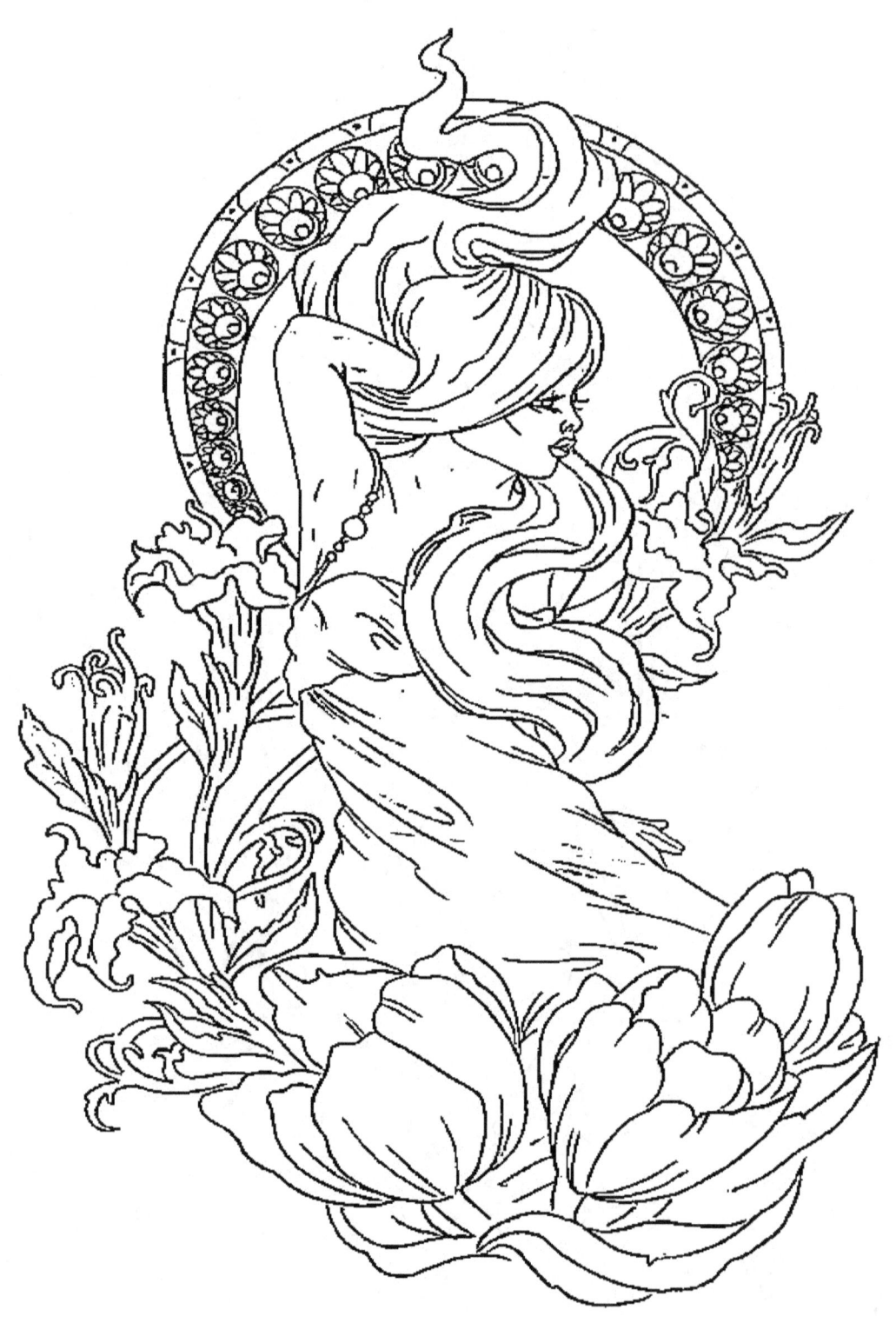

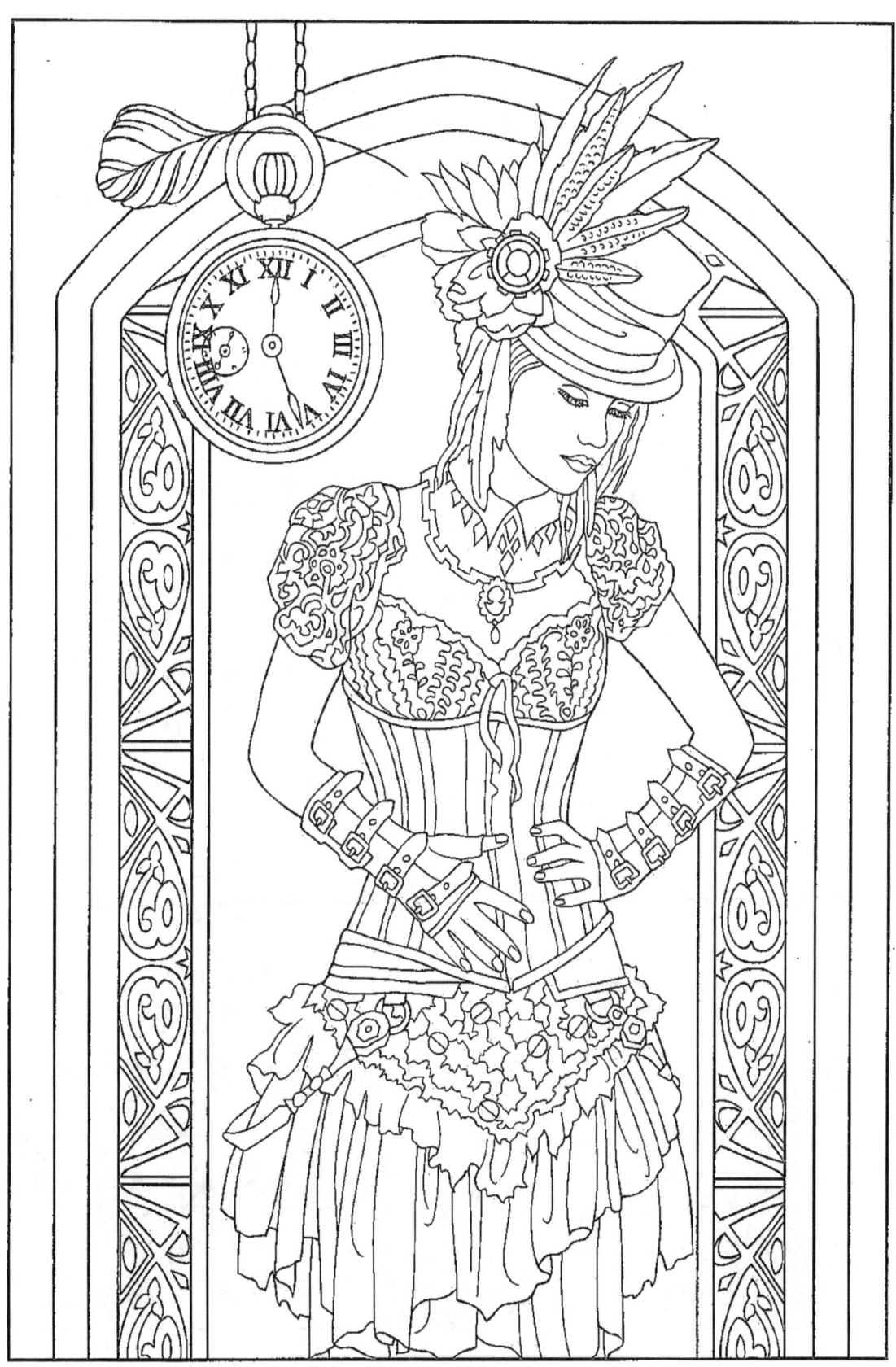

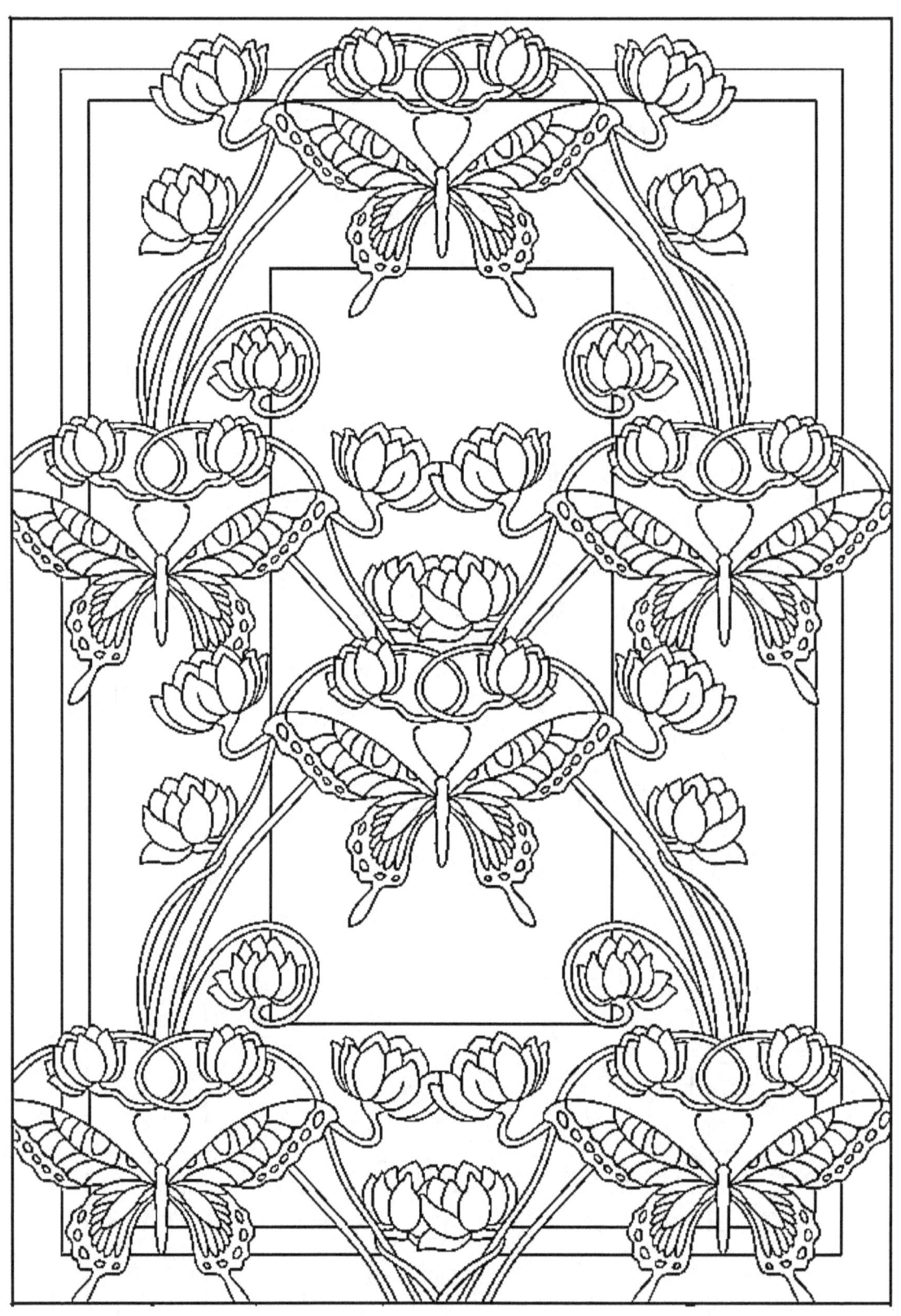

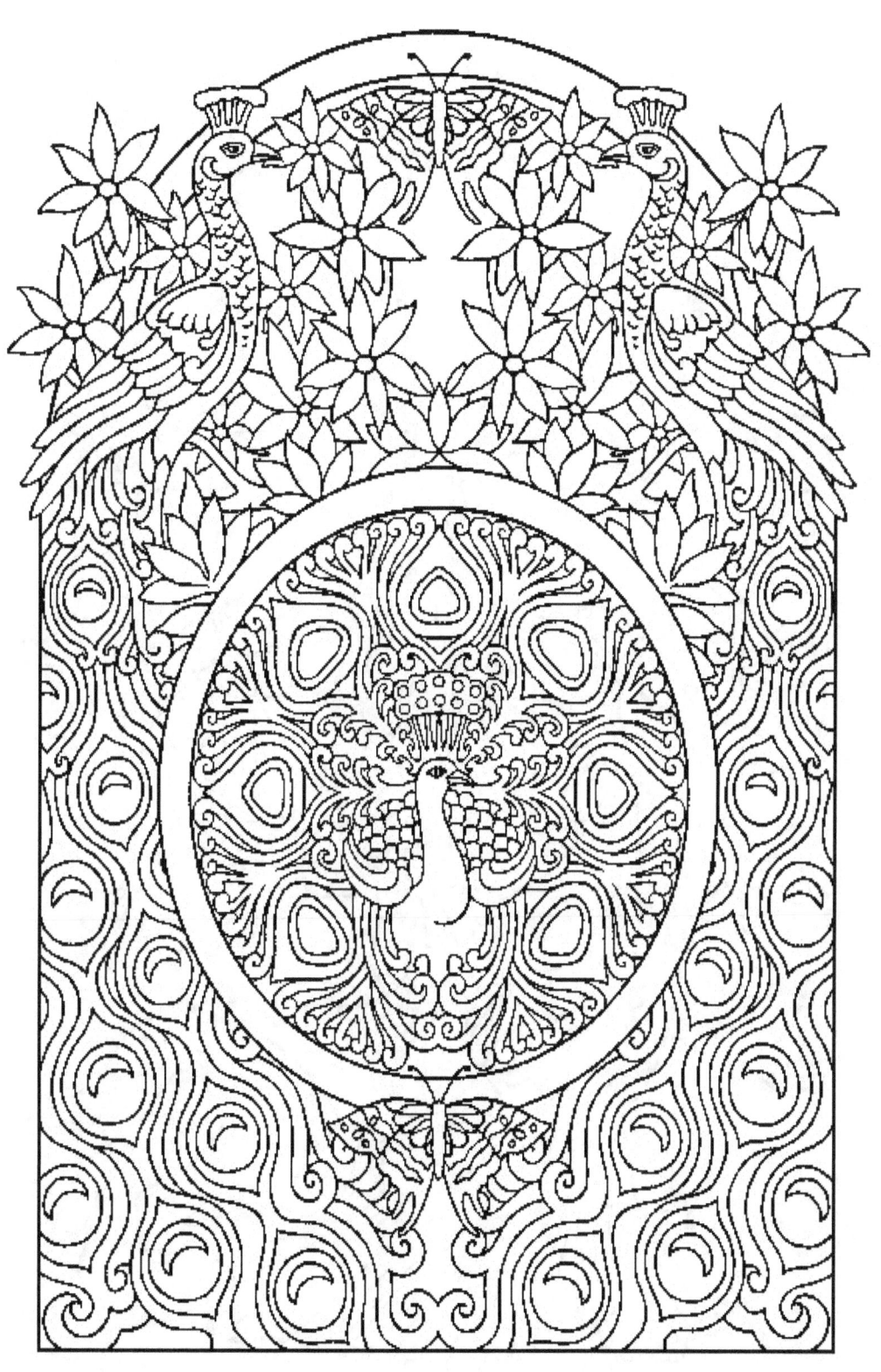

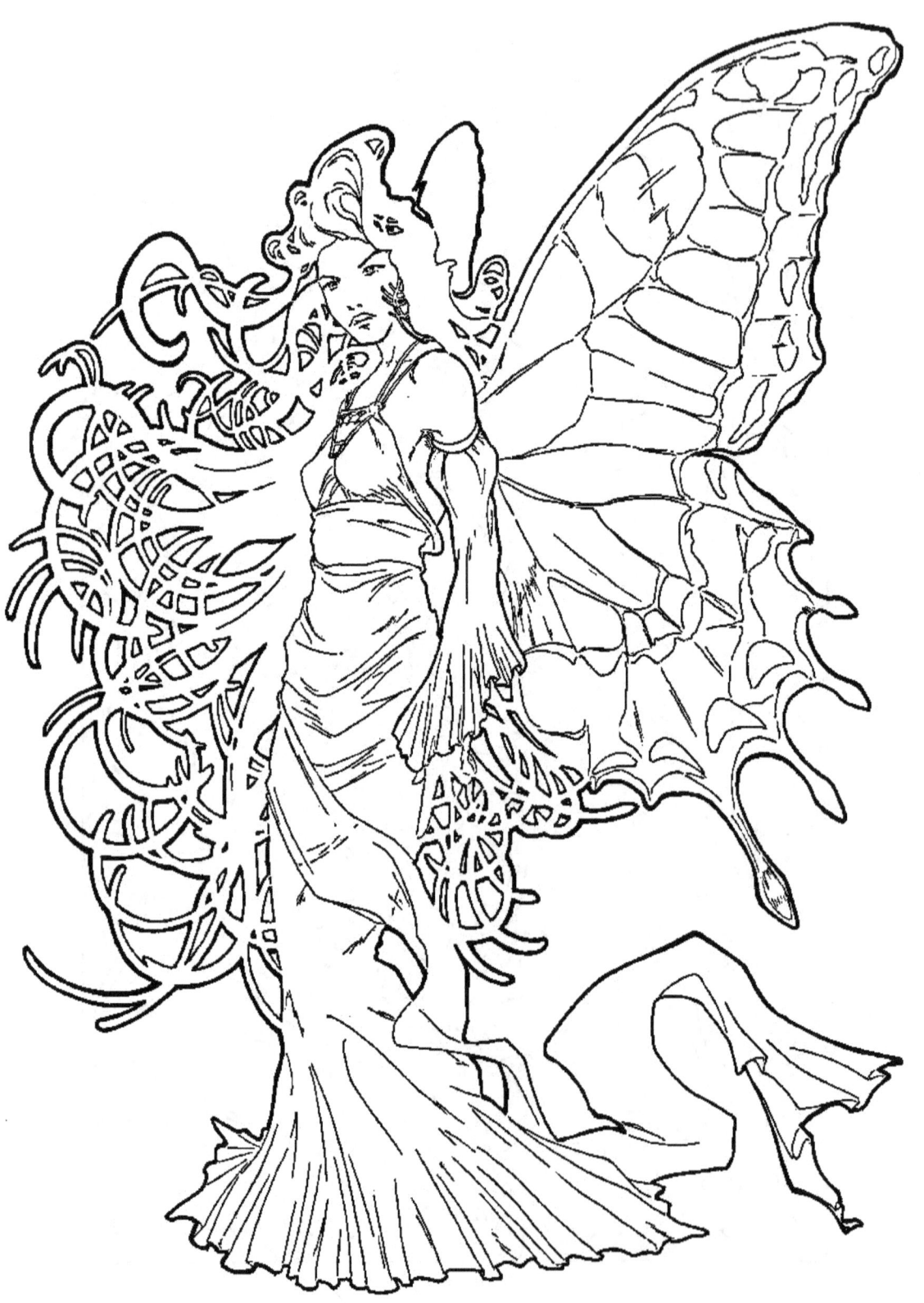

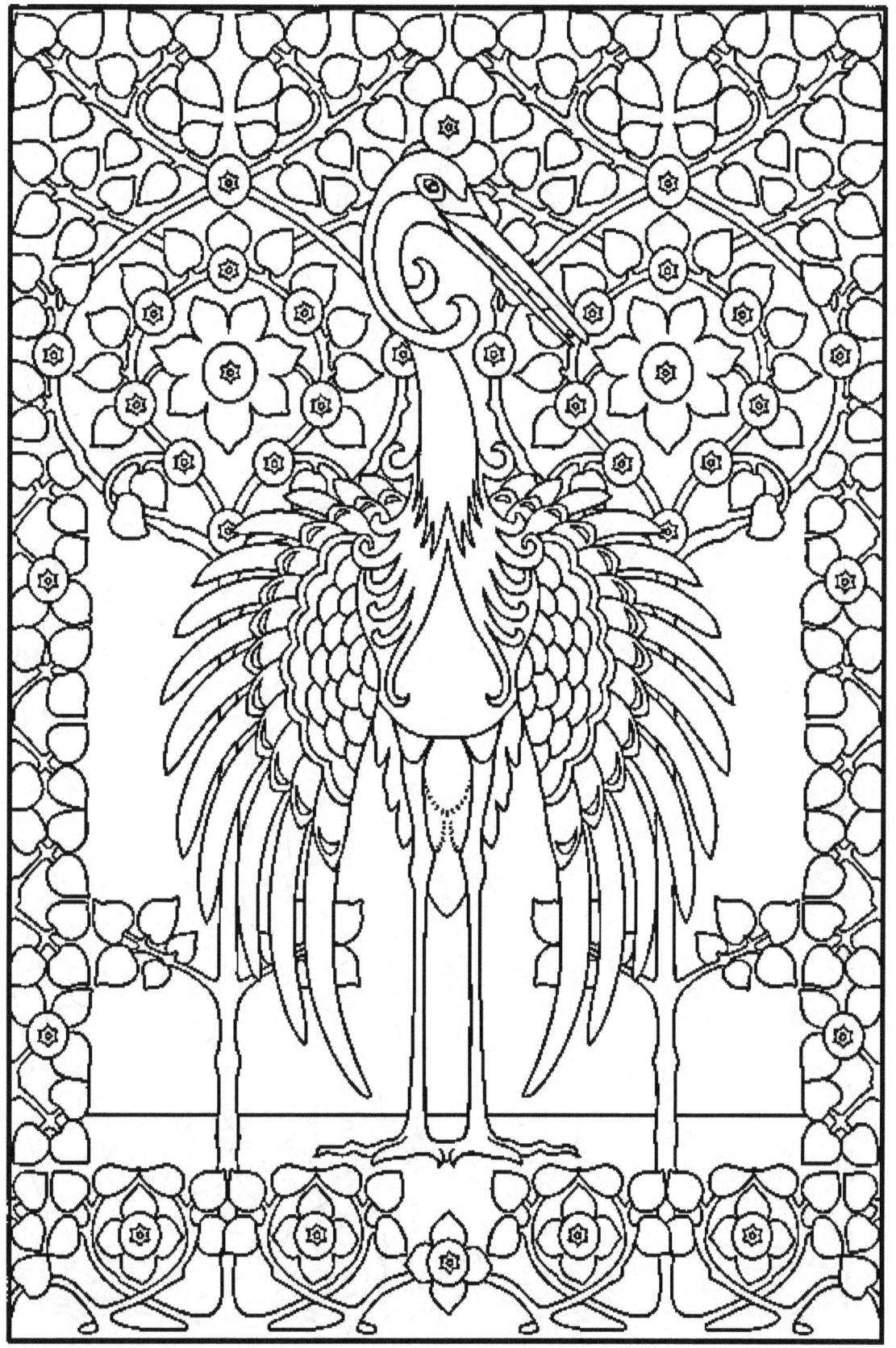

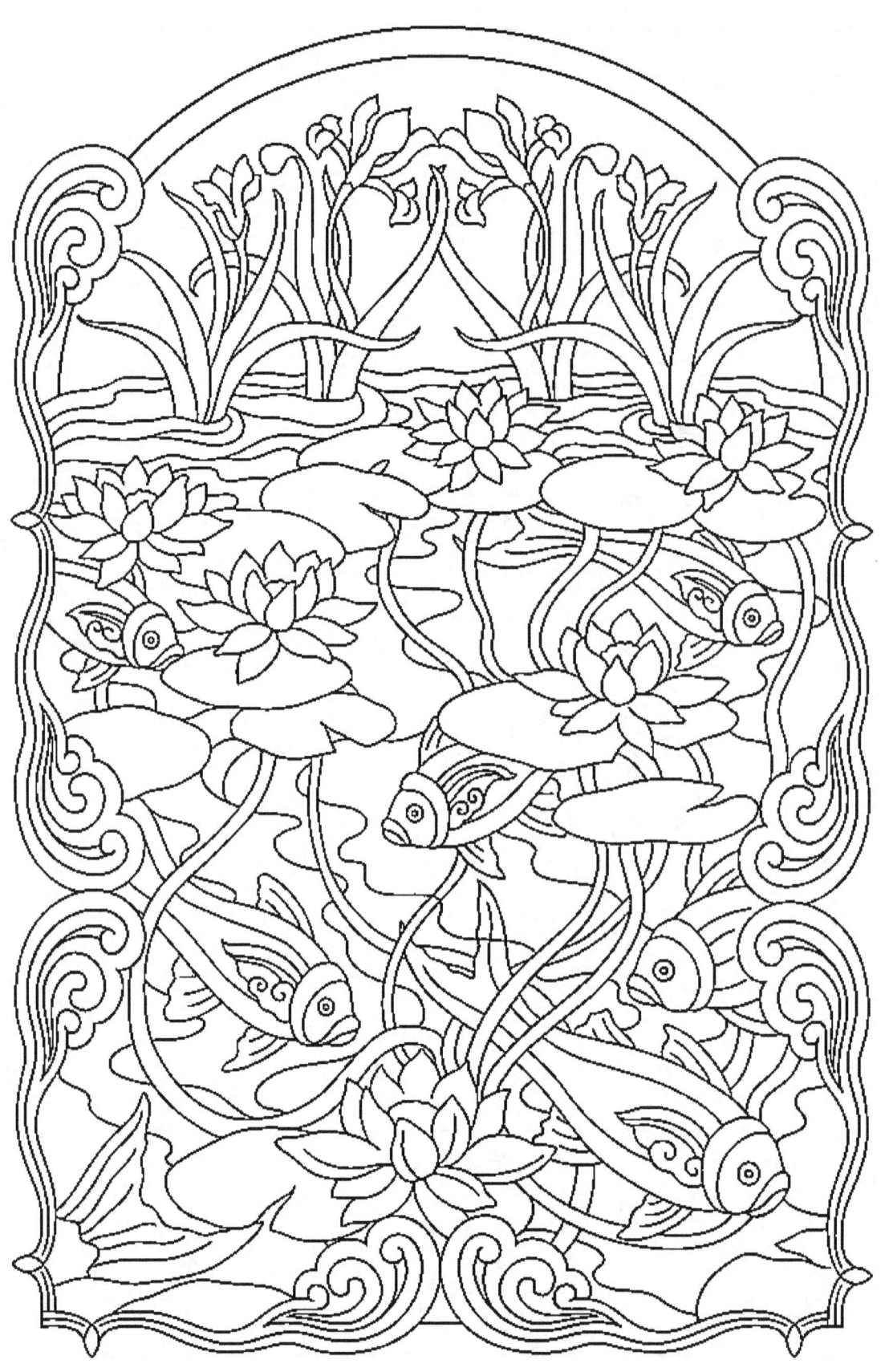

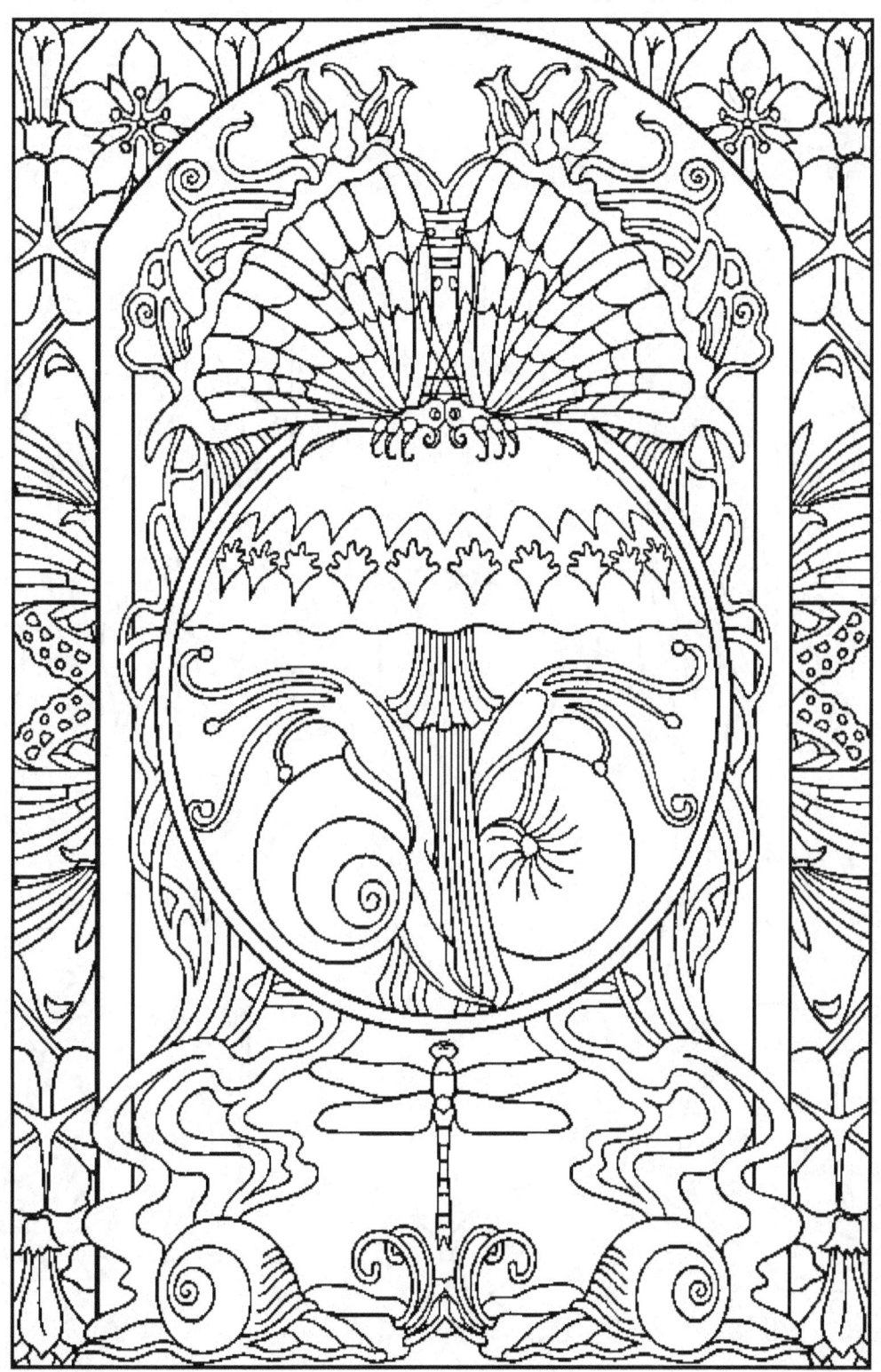

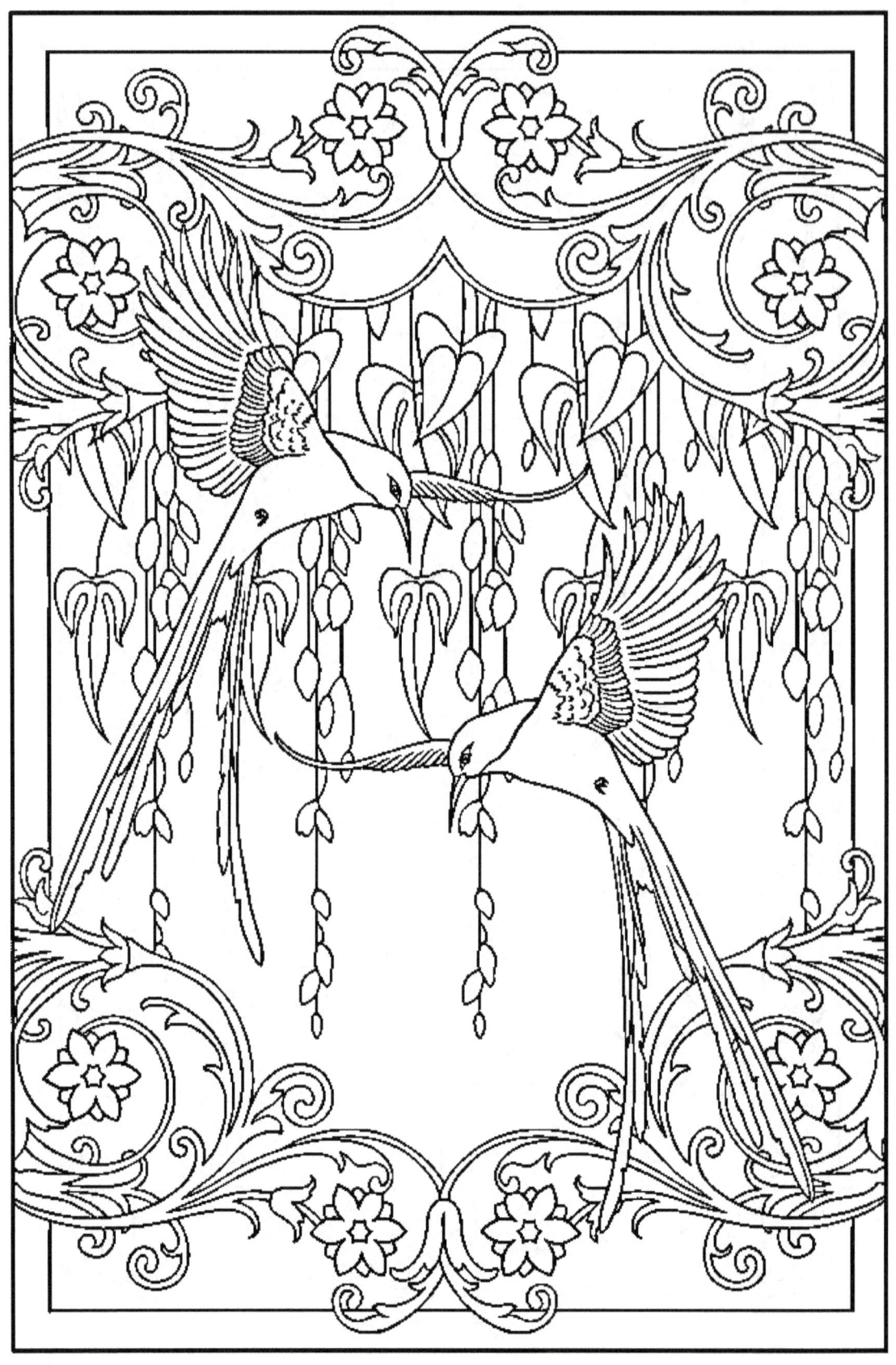

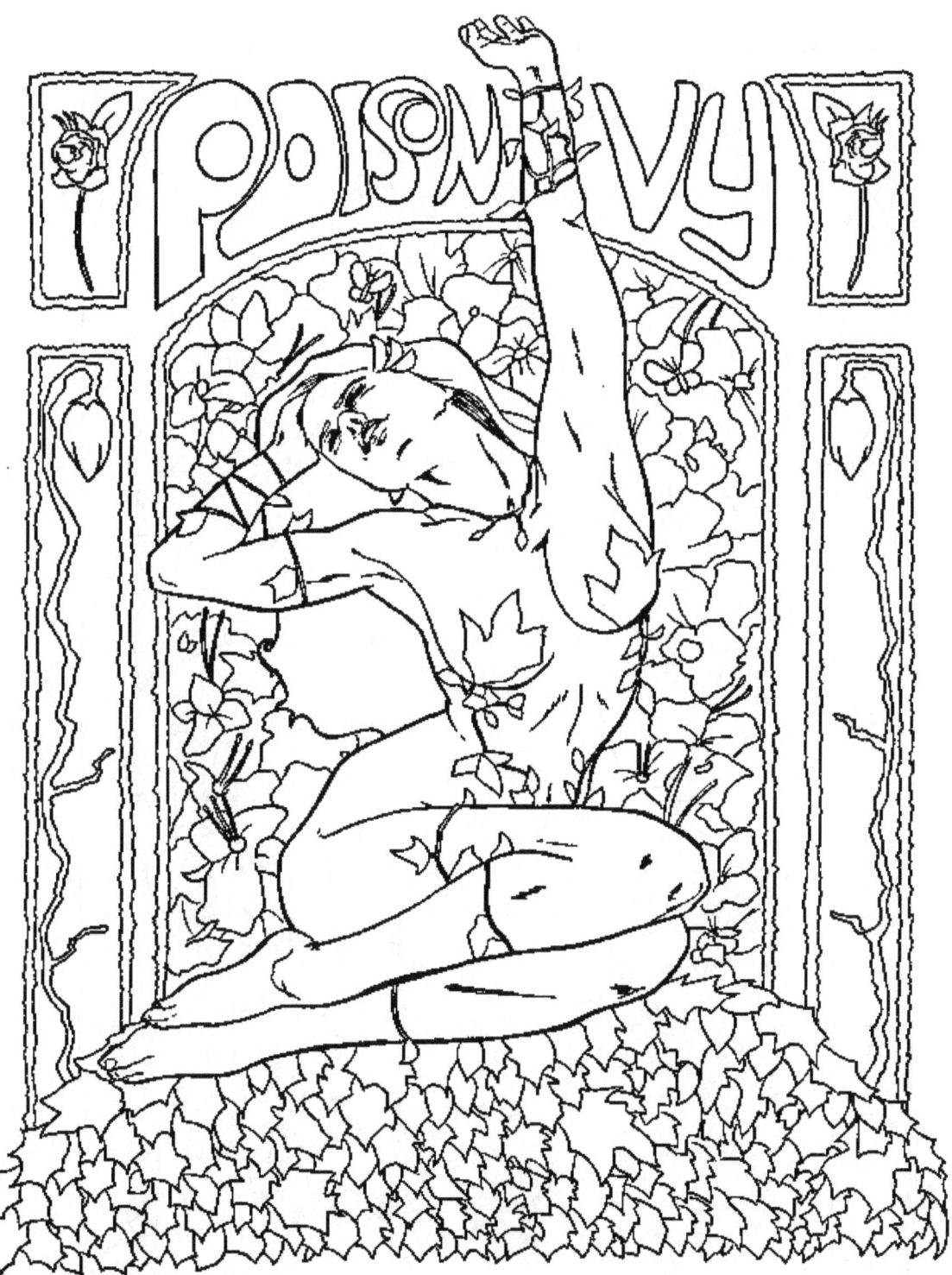

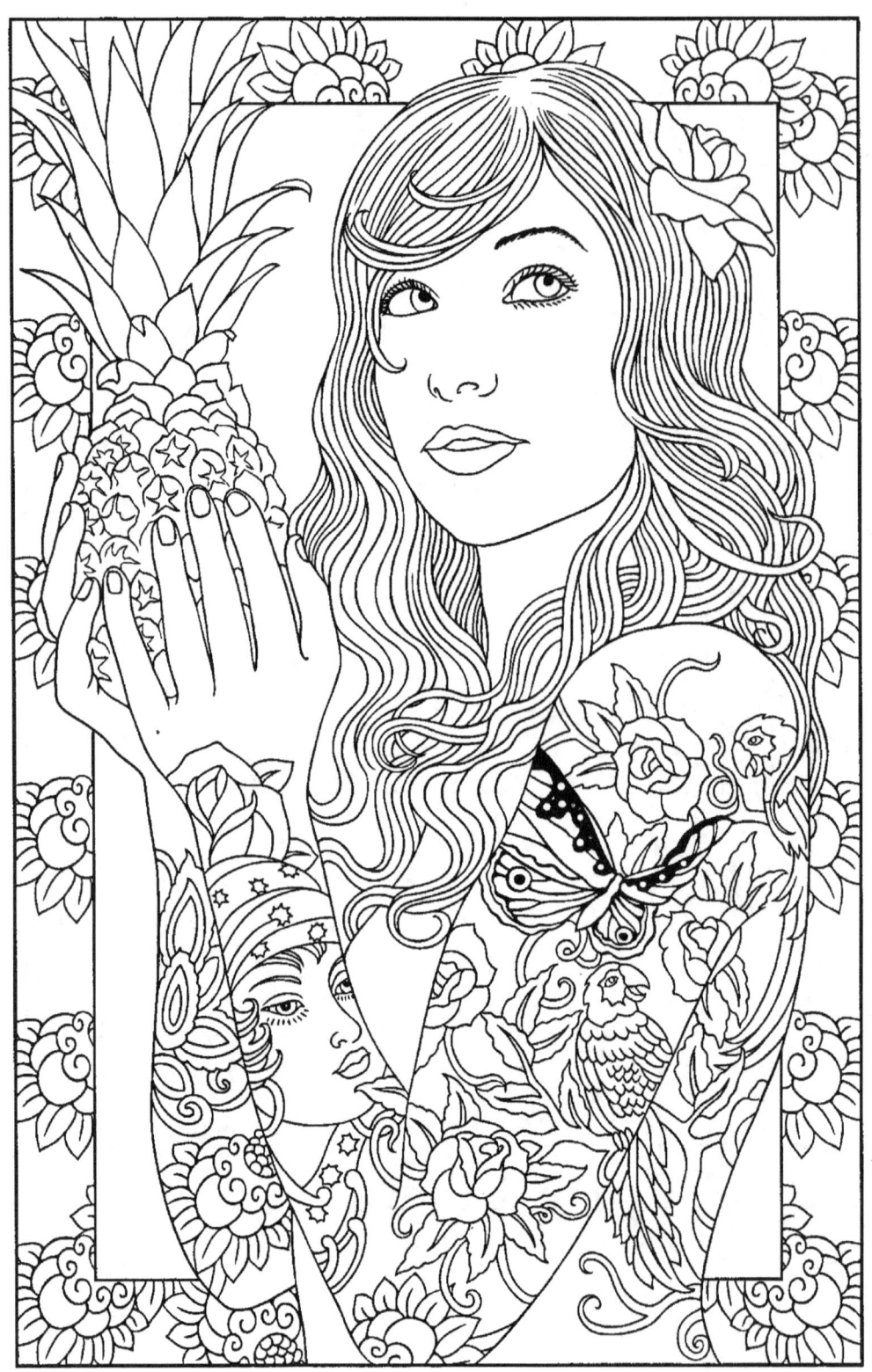

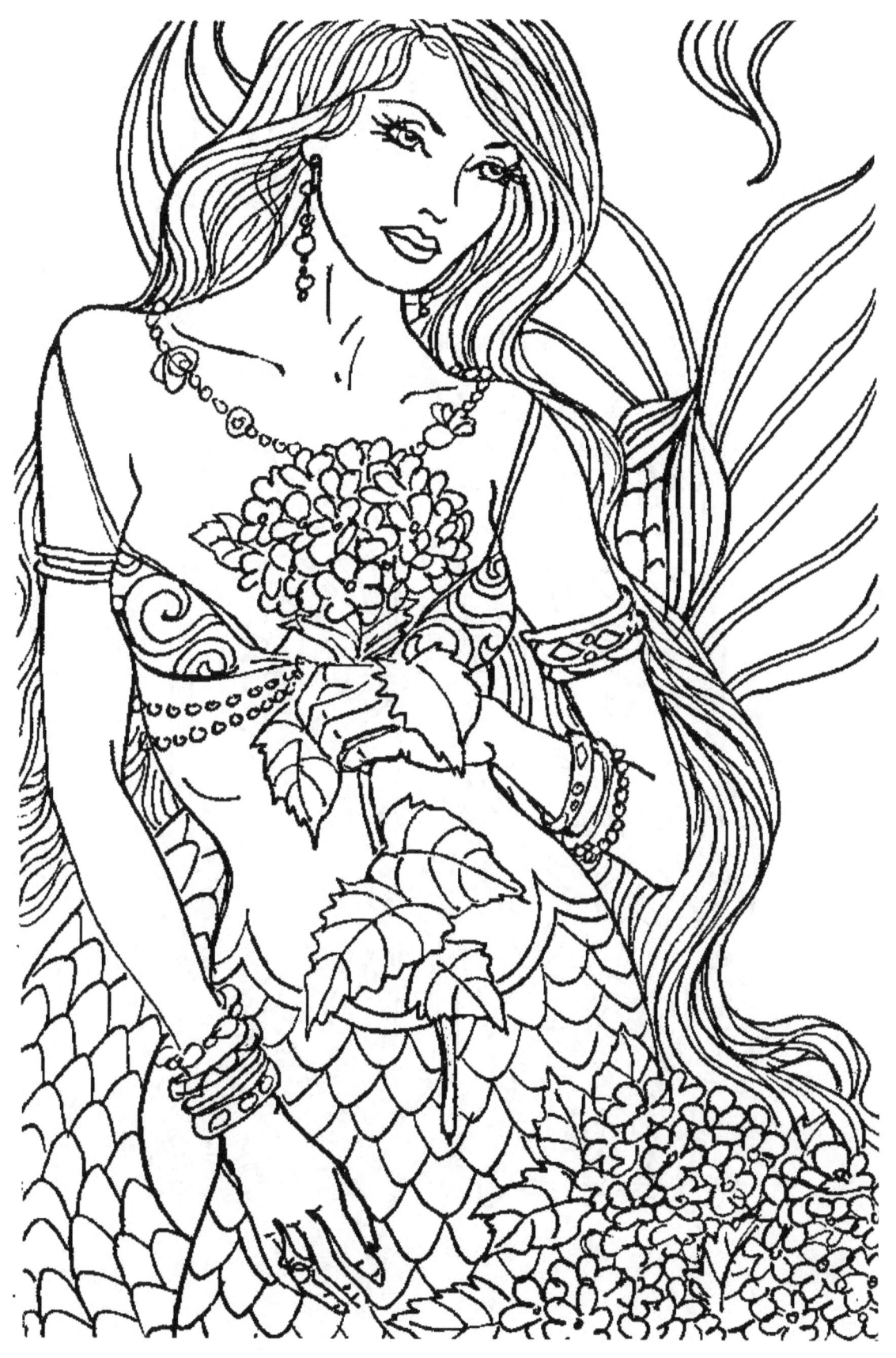

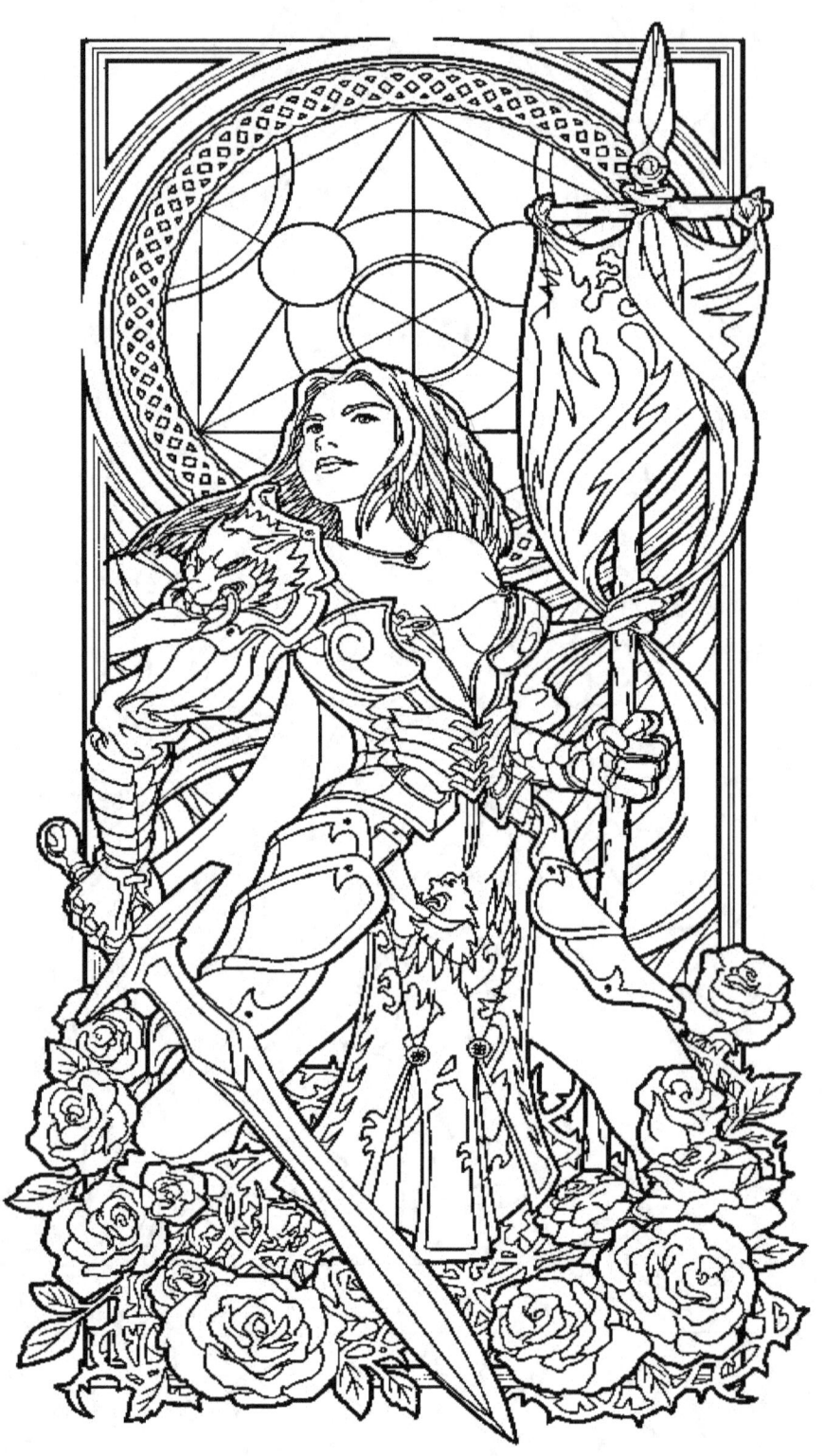

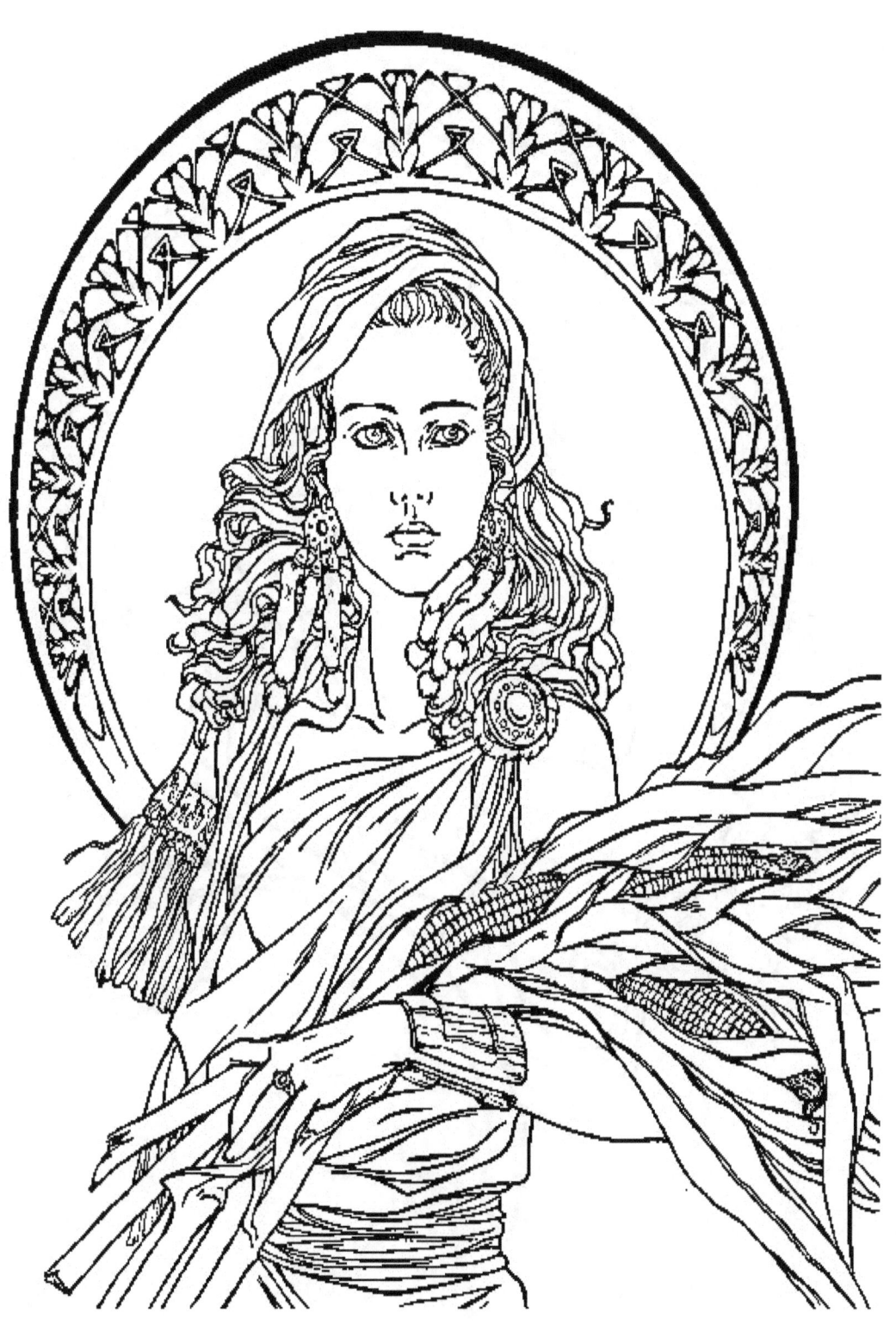

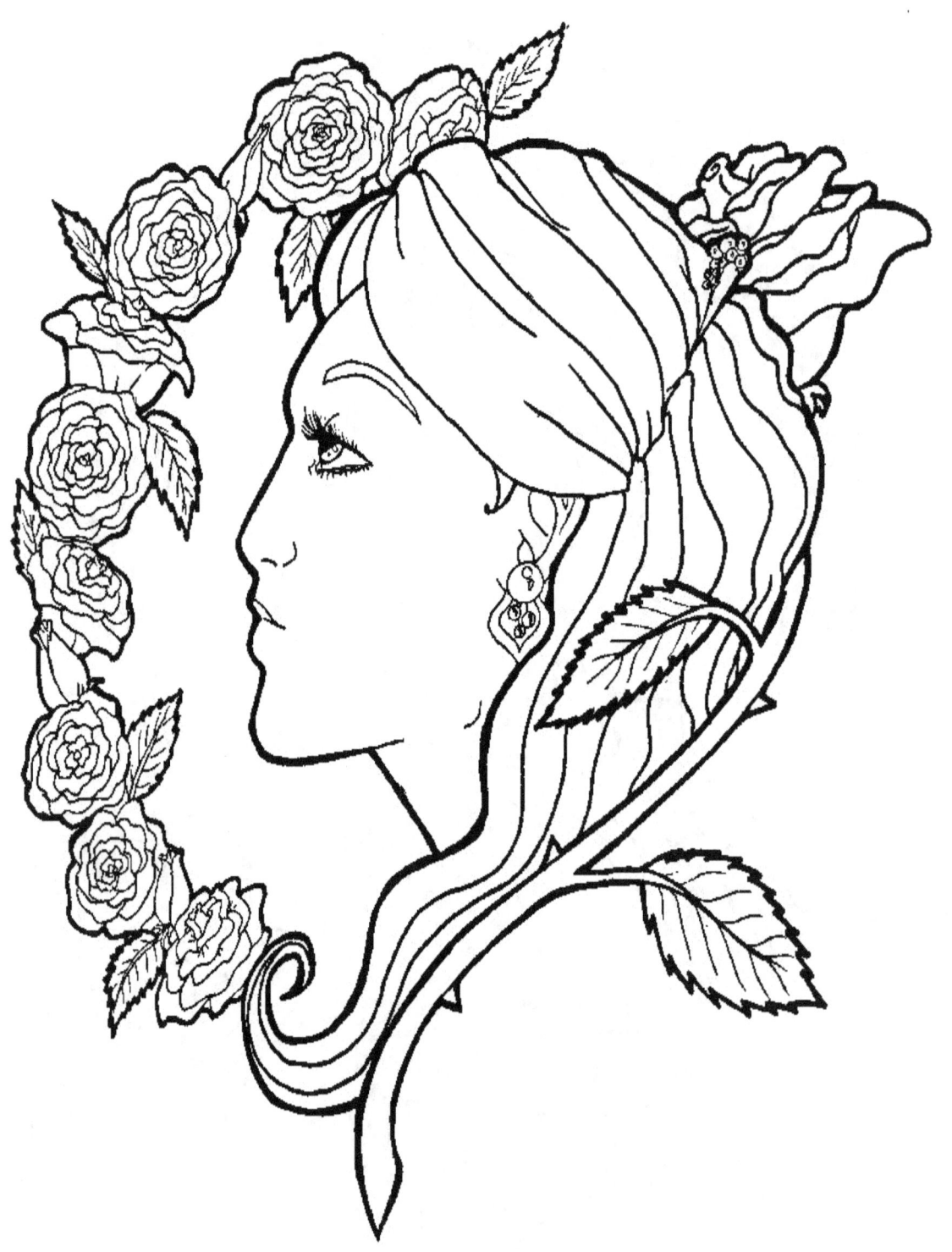

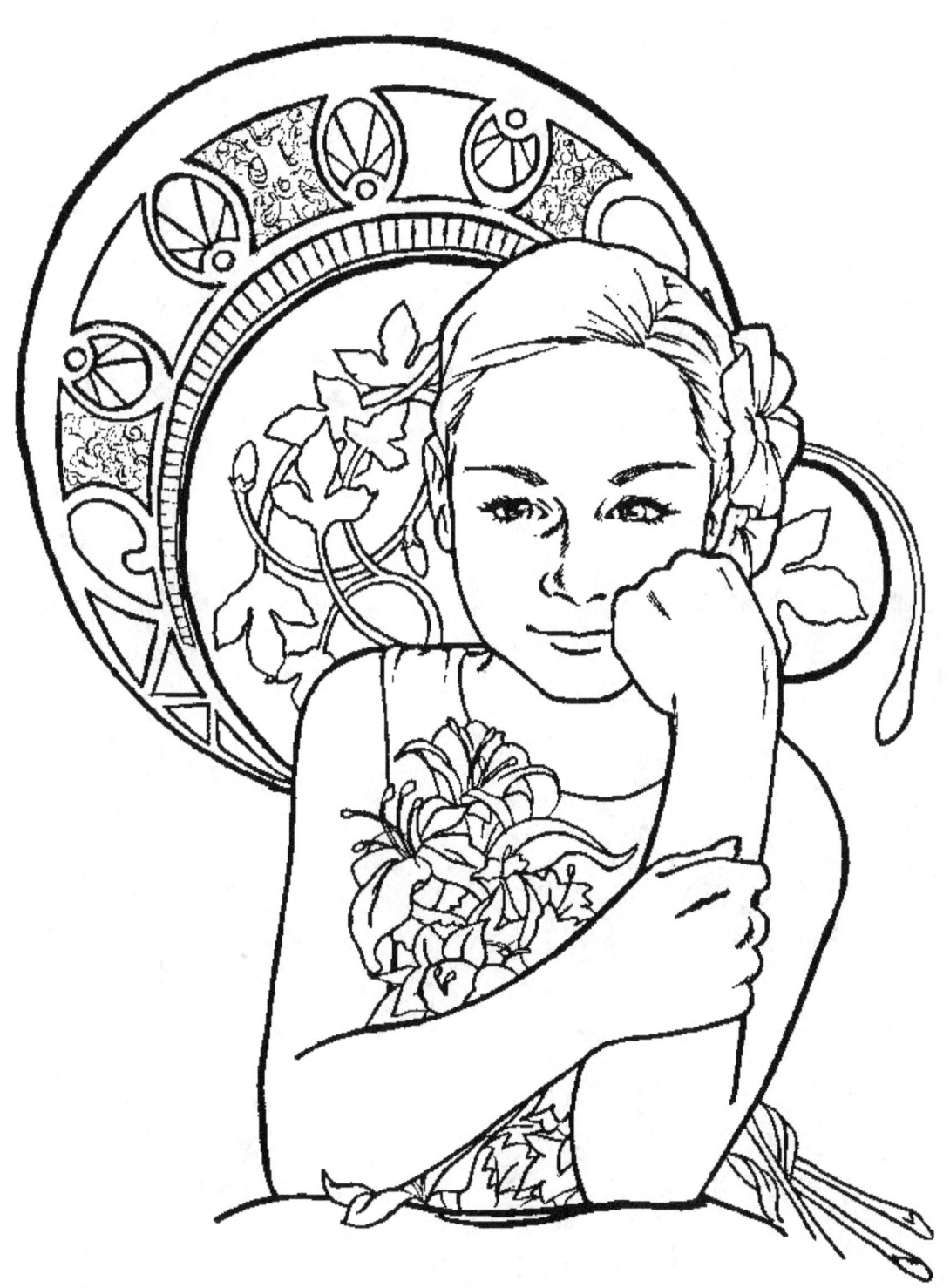

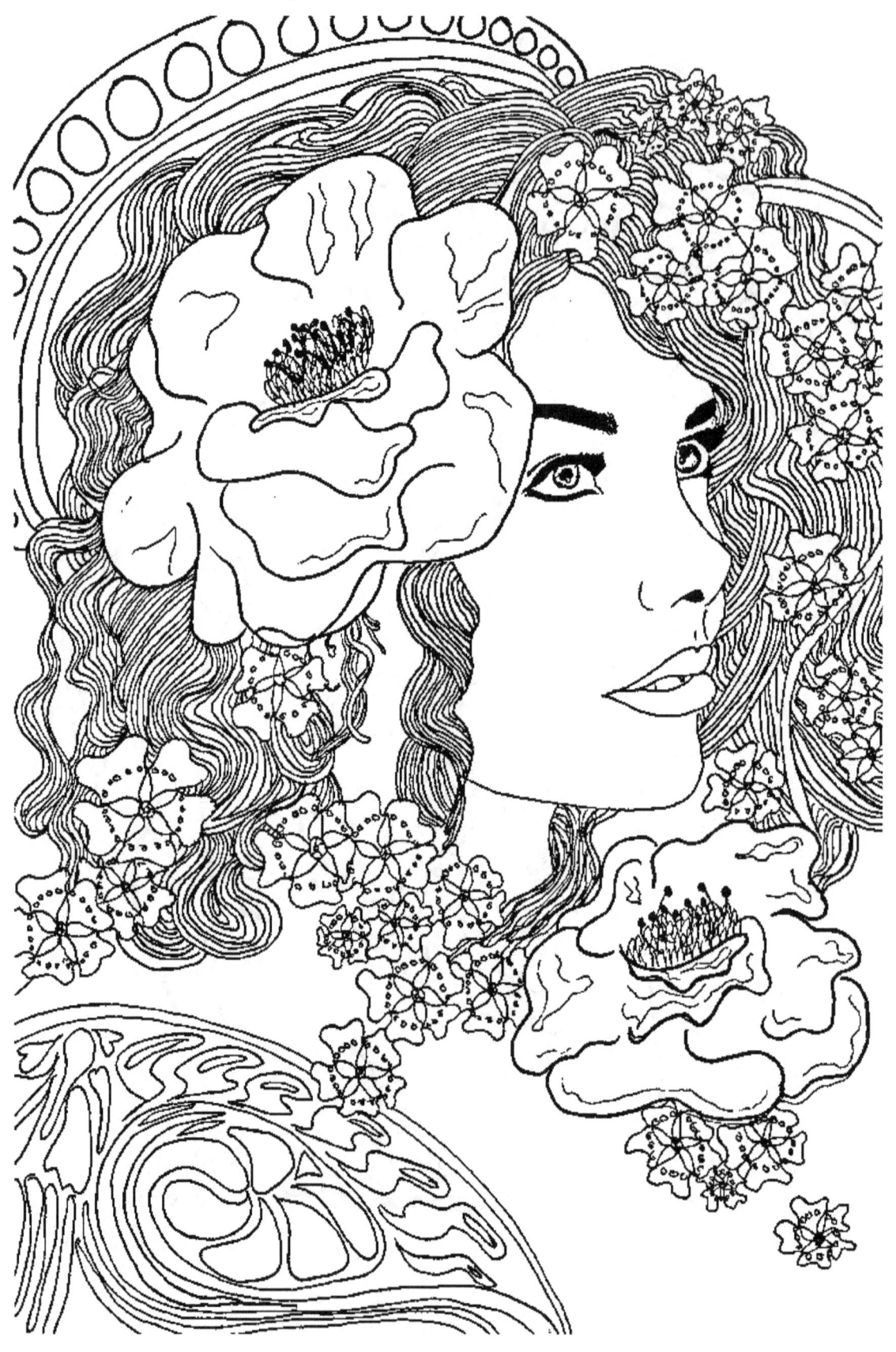